Grow 'Em Right

A Guide to Creating Habitat and Food Plots

Revised Edition

by

Neil & Craig Dougherty

Published by
NorthCountry Whitetails LLC
700 N. Main Street
Newark, NY 14513

Photos by NorthCountry Whitetails unless otherwise noted.
Cover Photo by Charles J. Alsheimer

ISBN: 0-9729356-1-4

Library of Congress Control Number: 2006923294

Printed in the United States Of America

DEDICATION

To

'KINDRED SPIRITS"

and
Bob "Gramps" Dougherty
for always being there.

"Conservation means harmony between men and land. When land does well for its owner and the owner does well by his land, when both end up better by reason of their partnership, we have conservation."

— Aldo Leopold

Contents

Dedication iii

Acknowledgments vi

Foreword by Charlie Alsheimer vii

Chapter I   Why We Wrote This Book 11

Chapter II   Getting Started...
               Make a Commitment, Develop a Plan 29

Chapter III   A Chainsaw is a Deer's Best Friend 47

Chapter IV   Property Access - Preventing and Creating 67

Chapter V   Logging Roads & Clearings 87

Chapter VI   Creating Sanctuaries 101

Chapter VII   Woods Working - TSI 111

Chapter VIII   Logging On 123

Chapter IX   Food Plots for Feeding 133

Chapter X   Food Plots for Hunting 151

Chapter XI   Planting by the Compass 173

Chapter XII   Big Toys for Big Boys (and Girls) 185

Chapter XIII   Selecting Cultivars for the Food Plot 199

Chapter XIV   Predicting Deer Movement: The
               Answer is Blow'n in the Wind 215

Chapter XV   Professional Property Layout 233

Chapter XVI   Quality Deer Hunting 251

Afterward 265

Acknowledgments

Many people assisted us with this book. They are all important to us and are deserving of our heartfelt thanks. They appear below in alphabetical order:

Aaron Alsheimer
Chris Asplundh
Kathy Balbierer and Kacey
Randy Bridge
Willis Brown
Dave & Beth Buckley
Kara Burd
Joe Byers
Peter Crawford
Bob "Gramps" Dougherty
Janet Dougherty
Laura Dougherty-Wilkins
Patrick Durkin
Peter & Kate Fiduccia
Bob Foulkrod
Brian Murphy
Laura & Charlie Palmer
Sharon Scholl & Erin
Jeff, Wayne & Steve Storie
Carl Whittier
Dr. Grant Woods

and

Charlie Alsheimer
for
Leading the Way

FOREWORD

Life is full of beginnings, with each new undertaking adding to life's total. In assessing my quarter-century as an outdoor communicator, I continually reflect on what has made my life a blessing beyond measure. Each new dawn, wildlife encounter and connection with another kindred spirit has played a significant role in my special journey.

I was born and raised in New York's Southern Tier potato region. From an early age, I had a bond with nature. Early on, this was manifested through hunting, which in time was enhanced by becoming a nature photographer and outdoor writer. It was only after I passed age 40 that I truly came to understand what stewarding the land is all about. In 1989, I traveled to South Texas to hunt and photograph. While there, I met the legendary Al Brothers, considered by many to be the father of the Quality Deer Management movement. He encouraged me to try and implement the QDM concept on my farm. I took Brother's words to heart and changed the way I had been managing the property.

For more than 10 years, I've been immersed in QDM. I admit there were times in the beginning I wasn't sure I was doing the right thing. This stemmed from skeptical reactions from fellow New Yorkers and the program's slow pace.

Traditions die hard in the Northeast and the thought of managing land for quality deer habitat and enjoyment was not an idea embraced by many New Yorkers in the early 1990s. Despite the drawbacks, I kept the vision and kept moving forward, thanks in large part to close friends and the successes we saw.

For years, I dreamed of the day quality bucks would walk the fields of western New York. It took time, but the day has arrived, thanks in large part to the vision of many like-minded individuals and landowners in our area. Two of the most inspirational have been my country neighbors and friends, Craig and Neil Dougherty.

Nearly a decade ago, I met Craig at the urging of fellow outdoor writer Bob Robb. At the time, I knew Craig as one of the "heavy hitters" in the hunting industry, but didn't know he owned property a scant seven air miles from my farm.

So, one sunny spring morning I drove from my farm to the top of the Catatunk, a forested hilltop region that sits on one of the highest points in Steuben County, New York. Craig and I had agreed to meet at his place after a morning of hunting gobblers on our respective properties. After the usual greetings, we sat in lawn chairs and sipped coffee next to his pop-up camper, while looking out over the beautiful Canisteo Valley.

The meeting was enlightening. For the better part of three hours, we discussed the outdoor industry, hunting, our families and what we were doing with our properties. At the time, I was a couple of years into managing our deer under the relatively new QDM concept that Al Brothers laid upon my heart in 1989. During our conversation, I learned Craig owned 150 acres, but had visions of adding more acreage and, as he put it, "Doing something more productive with it than just using it as place to hunt".

By the nature of the questions he asked that morning, I could tell he was intrigued by what I was trying to do with my property. Over the next three years, Craig, Neil and I had many fireside discussions concerning the pros and cons of quality deer management, as well as how to develop a property for both wildlife and hunting. It was obvious Craig and his son were excited by the prospects of what they could accomplish on their property, which they called "Kindred Spirits".

Over time they purchased more land, built a beautiful cabin, erected a conference center, and put their dream into motion. They involved wildlife/land management experts like Dave and Beth Buckley of West Valley, New York, Dr. Grant Woods and bowhunting expert Bob Foulkrod in an attempt to flatten the wildlife-management learning curve, and set up a state-of-the-art program. NorthCountry Whitetails Habitat Development and Hunting Demo Center was taking shape. As I watched what was growing, it was easy to see the Dougherty's had fallen in love with the concept of land management and quality deer hunting.

The result is that their vision has become a reality. It has taken time, but through much sweat and effort they've been able to put together a model 500-acre property that benefits both hunters and landowners.

It's safe to say their NorthCountry Whitetails Demo Center, located in rural Steuben County in New York, is a unique concept. It fact, with its tour program and conference center activities, it is the only one of its kind in the north to my knowledge. The practices and techniques they've developed have become the envy of nearly every land owner and hunter who has been introduced to their style of land/wildlife management. Hundreds have learned the "how-to's" of habitat management and food plots from visiting the operation.

Now they've taken their program to the next level by sharing how they did it in the book you are holding. If you are looking for a "how-to" volume on creating a white-tailed deer Mecca that benefits habitat, all wildlife and the hunter, this is it. If you are struggling with how to turn your land or hunting lease into something better, this book can show you how to do it. In short, this book is a down-to-earth, step-by-step volume on how to cut your losses and reap big gains in the shortest length of time.

For too long, many have viewed the concept of land development and quality deer management as something complicated. Although it can be difficult if not done properly, pulling it off is not rocket science. *Grow "Em Right: A Guide to Creating Habitat and Food Plots*, will show you how to obtain the results you are dreaming about in the least amount of time.

So, sit back and let the Dougherty's lead you on a cutting edge wildlife journey, the likes of which you've probably never experienced. If you're like me, you'll be a better steward for having done so.

Charlie Alsheimer
Northern Field Editor
Deer and Deer Hunting *Magazine*

Chapter I

Why We Wrote This Book

Neil and Steve charged through the cabin door, their eyes as big as saucers. They couldn't wait to tell Craig and bowhunting legend Bob Foulkrod what they had just seen. Dressed in T-shirts for the unseasonably hot weather, they had spent midday scouting a seldom-hunted area. They were about 75 yards apart in thick cover, but each got a close look at a majestic white-tailed buck as it dogged a doe. The buck's 20-inch spread made them confident it would make "the book" with plenty to spare. This deer was the biggest buck either had seen on the property. It wasn't many years ago that any buck got the boys in this Steuben County, New York camp excited. But things have improved dramatically since then.

Minutes later, the four hunters held a meeting to craft a hunting strategy. The encounter with the big buck occurred in terrain near "The Hole", a steep, thick semi-sanctuary they rarely hunted. Rather than risk spooking the buck from the area, they set up stands near the site's perimeter, hoping to catch him coming out after does.

Neil Dougherty got this 136 Pope-and-Young buck five years after he and his father, Craig, decided to practice "quality deer hunting" on their property in Steuben County, New York. Neil and Craig progressed from shooting spikes, forkhorns and small 6-pointers to record-book deer. They now routinely see bucks like this one.

For the rest of the weekend, the hunters focused their effort on "The Big One". Gone was the need for instant success. They tried to understand their quarry's habits and get in position for a shot. On the weekend's last sit, Neil spotted the buck again as it left "The Hole" with its' nose to the ground. The buck obviously had does on the brain.

The deer walked past Neil's stand about 40 yards upwind, hit a clover-covered logging road, and turned uphill. It was moving steadily along the road and would pass through a shooting lane at about 30 yards. When the buck walked behind a mass of grape vines, Neil drew his bow. The release was true and the arrow found its mark.

Neil waited a half-hour until he could stand the suspense no longer. After climbing down and investigating, he found his blood-

covered arrow. Minutes later, 75 yards along the trail, he spotted brown, and then the antlers. The 136 Pope-and-Young buck lay still in the leaves. Neil couldn't wait to tell everyone. Craig, Neil's father, had already departed because of a business obligation. He heard the story via his cell phone after landing at a Florida airport.

Since that day, Neil's buck has been written about in several hunting magazines, not because of its size - it's not outstanding as book-bucks go - but because of what it represents. Neil's big buck came after eight years of intensive quality deer hunting and habitat-development work at NorthCountry's 500-acre property in hunter-dense Steuben County, New York. Neil's buck represented a defining moment. We had taken a trophy buck from our property, a feat we once thought impossible. Our habitat development and quality deer-hunting program was working! Neil's buck was a perfect case-study of how to improve deer hunting on a typical woodland property.

The Demo Center is Born

Today, the same property - which routinely produces record-book bucks - is more than a hunting property. It has been converted into the only Demo Center of its kind open to the public in the United States. It is 500 acres of prime deer habitat, much of it created through habitat-development projects over the past 16 years. It also serves as the field headquarters of the Whitetail Alliance, an organization founded by NorthCountry Whitetails and The Whitetail Institute of North America. With over 40 acres of real world and experimental food plots and hundreds of acres additional habitat management projects, it is a showcase of whitetail management practices. Best of all, it offers a host of educational programs to the public. It even contains a Conference Center designed to accommodate meetings, seminars, and other indoor activities.

The Demo Center has been featured on dozens of television programs, in DVDs and written about in numerous books, newspa-

Neil Dougherty, fourth from the right, discusses food plots with a tour group visiting the NorthCountry Whitetails Demo Center. Each year, Neil leads hundreds of visitors through the 500-acre property. Many are landowners setting out on their own quality deer hunting endeavor.

pers and magazines. With more than 50 percent of all licensed deer hunters living within an eight-hour drive of the facility, it has been visited by thousands of whitetail enthusiasts over the past 5 years.

The Book

The second edition of this book, like the first, is organized around the Demo Center's tours. The second edition is fully updated and reflects most of what we have learned since writing the first edition. The new information is imbedded in first edition chapters and in three entirely new chapters. A great deal of new information has hit the whitetail habitat and food plot industry in the past three years. We believe we have included the most important findings in this edition. We have also included more advanced information in this edition. The questions coming from the public sector have changed. Our readers are asking higher-level questions that demand more sophisticated answers and discussions. We have

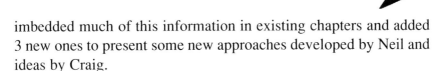

imbedded much of this information in existing chapters and added 3 new ones to present some new approaches developed by Neil and ideas by Craig.

Our book is not about theory. It's about practice. It's about what has worked for us, and what we know will work for you. Our book, like our tours, emphasizes a balanced approach to quality deer hunting and habitat development. It's about total property management, not just food plots. It's about creating quality wildlife habitat and quality deer hunting. It addresses the everyday problems and questions of the thousands of habitat-development enthusiasts we talk with each year. These questions include:

1   "What can I do about trespassers?"

2   "How do I get my neighbors to cooperate?"

3   "How can I set up my property to hold mature whitetail bucks?"

4   "How do I set up a sanctuaries and food plots?"

5   "What can I expect if I clear-cut a patch of woods?"

6   "How much lime and fertilizer should I apply, and how should I apply it?"

7   "What deer forages work best in what locations?"

8   "How do I keep my food plots producing for five years or more?"

9   "What equipment do I need?"

10   "How should I hunt my property?"

This book discusses what works, what doesn't, and how we progressed from rookie habitat managers to creators of one of the country's finest examples of whitetail range.

Creating Quality Whitetail Hunting

This book is also about creating quality whitetail hunting. In the late 1980s, we dreamed about having our own place to hunt whitetails. By the early 1990s, we dreamed of seeing trophy bucks on our property. By 2000, our dreams had become reality. By 2005 we had trained thousand of others to do the same.

Our Demo Center is the heart and soul of our operation. It's where we do our research, test new products, produce TV and DVDs, and develop ideas for books and magazine articles. It is where we meet with the whitetail enthusiasts who visit our facility almost every weekend; the ones just starting out or well into their program, often asking, "I've always dreamed about having quality deer hunting. How do I make it happen?"

These Steuben County trophies were taken within 48 hours of each other from two separate New York properties, both of which follow practices outlined in this book. Ten years ago, a photo like this would have shown forkhorns, 6-pointers and maybe a basket 8-pointer. Today, whitetails this size are seen regularly on our properties.

Above all, this book strives to help others realize their dreams. We believe a quality deer hunting experience is within the grasp of almost anyone who works hard, is willing to learn, and wants it enough to dare to dream. Our Demo Center tours and Whitetail Alliance short courses have helped thousands of deer hunters get closer to living their dream.

The Book is Based on Experience

We've tried every plan and technique we write about in this book. This book is not a review of scientific research or a compilation of telephone interviews with experts. It is a hands-on book about hands-on projects and practices. But, make no mistake: It's not all about what we "learned the hard way", far from it. Since the early 1990s, we have worked with the top experts in the business.

Neil took these two "book-bucks" within 24 hours of each other from the same food plot. The smaller buck was taken on the last afternoon of New York's archery season. The bigger buck was taken the next day during the first afternoon of gun season. Both bucks were checking out does feeding on snow-covered brassica.

Each of them has spent time at the Demo Center, working and hunting beside us. You can see the influence of our group of experts on projects all over the Demo Center. We know of no other property that has received so much attention from so many leaders in hunting and wildlife management. Each brings a specific set of knowledge and skills, and each complements the others.

Leading Experts in the Field

We have been blessed to work with some of the best hunting and habitat-development professionals in the country. They have been our mentors and our friends.

Charlie Alsheimer, arguably one of the best whitetail photographers in North America, is an expert on deer behavior. He spends lots of time with a herd of white-tailed deer he keeps on his Steuben County farm in New York. When he's not photographing and studying whitetails, Charlie is busy writing about them.

Our good friend, Charles Alsheimer, who started us down the quality deer-hunting path, is one of North America's top white-tailed deer behaviorists and, arguably, its best whitetail photographer. Many of Charlie's photos appear in this book. Charlie has been a pioneer in quality deer management in the North, and is responsible for showing thousands of hunters the way with his multi-media shows and seminars. He is also the host of *Deer and Deer Hunting TV*. He reaches thousands of hunters with his spectacular books including *Quality Deer Management: The Basics and Beyond*. Many habitat projects at our Demo Center were done with Charlie's help. He has been a source of encouragement, helping us "stay the course" since the early 1990s, years when we weren't always confident of our new approach. We continue to conduct research together and exchange information daily.

Dr. Grant Woods has contributed immeasurably to NorthCountry's understanding of deer nutrition and all growing things. Grant, a wildlife researcher, author, and consultant, manages hundreds of thousands of acres of wildlife properties for his clients which include some of the world's finest hunting operations.

Dr. Grant Woods manages hundreds of thousands of acres of deer habitat for his clients in North America.

Grant frequently appears on TV and is a sought after speaker. He has been instrumental to the success of the Quality Deer Management Association and has been a friend to NorthCountry Whitetails for almost 20 years.

Dave and Beth Buckley, friends from western New York, are pioneers in habitat development. They are part of a rare group of individuals who have been doing this 30 or more years. They are willing teachers and stewards of the land. Their property is a model of habitat development. The Buckley's helped enormously to develop the facility during its early years. Their advice started us on the correct path and kept us there ever since. We always learn something from the Buckley's when we hit the field together.

Dave and Beth Buckey are naturalists who have been creating quality deer habitat for more than 30 years. They started the Doughertys down the habitat-development path in the early 1990s, and continue to offer them expert advice.

Bob Foulkrod makes his living by hunting. He is considered by many deer hunters to be the best in the business at reading terrain and setting up effective stand sites. He has seen it all, learning something from every one of his thousands of hunts. Many hunting setups at the Demo Center were created by Bob, Neil and Charlie Alsheimer.

Bob Foulkrod is a regular at our Demo Center and hunts the property whenever he can. Bob has been a hunting mentor to Neil since he was old enough to draw a bow. As thousands know, Bob is the ultimate bowhunting machine. His occupation as a professional hunter - almost always in front of a camera - requires proficiency in hunting new terrain. He is the master of reading property and setting up for a kill. He has greatly assisted Neil in putting together world-class hunting setups at the Demo Center. These setups, and other hunting strategies from our team of experts, can be viewed by those who visit the Demo Center.

This book's authors are a father-son team with a shared passion for hunting and habitat development. Their skills and experiences, while unique, are highly complementary.

Craig's background is in research and education. In fact, he was a teacher and university professor for more than a dozen years.

One of Craig's passions is business and organizational development, especially in the hunting industry. For more than 25 years he has been involved in hunter education, combating anti-hunters, and growing the sports of archery and bowhunting. He was Vice-President and Vice-Chairman of Bear Archery, and Golden Eagle Archery. He has served as Chairman of the National Board of Directors of the Quality Deer Management Association and is the Executive Director of the Whitetail Alliance. He is on a first-name basis with most of the big names in the hunting industry; he has hunted and worked on industry and conservation projects with many of them. He serves on many industry steering committees.

Neil has grown up around the hunting industry's leaders. He has shared campfires with the likes of Bob Foulkrod, Chuck

Bob Foulkrod, Neil Dougherty and Charlie Alsheimer discuss stand-location strategies at NorthCountry's Demo Center. Visitors to the center see this exact setup and others conceived by the pros. Neil, shown here in the center, presents this setup and others to the public in his magazine articles and hunting seminars.

Adams, and Jerry Martin. He has worked professionally with Alsheimer and Dr. Woods. In short, Neil has been trained by the best of the best, and it shows in his work.

In addition to running the Demo Center, Neil presents about 50 seminars across the country each year and is a featured presenter at most of the Quality Deer Management Association's National Conventions. He also writes for several outdoor magazines, and appears frequently on television. He produced NorthCountry's DVD, Plant' Em Right. He has been profiled in many books and magazines and is generally considered to be one of the top young deer experts in the country.

He is a wildlife habitat consultant and currently manages over 100,000 acres of prime deer hunting properties. Neil still finds time to hunt, which remains his passion and is best known for his ability to use his technical training and sixth sense for deer to set up properties for maximum hunting success.

· ·

We have taken thousands of people through our outdoors classroom. But we realize not everyone can visit the Demo Center. This book brings the Center to our readers.

· ·

Neil teaches many of the courses offered by the Whitetail Alliance. He also serves as a research and wildlife habitat development specialist for the Whitetail Institute of North America.

Together, the authors have built a company - NorthCountry Whitetails - that's dedicated to providing the products, services and education necessary to create quality deer hunting.

We have taken thousands of people through our outdoors classroom. But we realize not everyone can visit the Demo Center. This book brings the Center to our readers.

The public can view the results of countless years of learning and teaching by the best deer experts in the world at our Demo Center. The same information is also found in the pages of this book.

Our Mission is Education

Our decision to open the Demo Center and invite the public inside for tours, "demo days" and workshops did not come lightly. It's one thing to write articles about our projects and appear on television occasionally, but it's another to invite public participation. We value our privacy and knew the human traffic required to share our knowledge and passion for habitat development would probably affect the hunting we cherish. However, the joy of seeing others move closer to realizing their dreams has become an important part of our lives. We are lucky to have learned from the best in the

The NorthCountry Whitetails habitat development tour covers about six miles and lasts about four hours. The tractor-drawn tram allows visitors to relax and enjoy while learning basic and advanced habitat concepts. It stops at about 20 demo areas, including habitat projects, food plots and hunting setups.

country, and believe others should have the same chance. We share our knowledge and help others develop successful programs. And we do mean successful! Since the early 1990s, every aspect of our hunting experience has improved, and the age structure and size of the deer on our property has increased. Friends and followers of the methods in this book experience similar success.

All Demo Center land is free range. It contains no pens or deer proof fenced enclosures. We started with 150 acres and now control more than 500 acres. The neighbors on all sides of the Demo Center hunt, but not everyone subscribes to quality deer hunting practices. In fact, one group would be considered poor hunting neighbors. But that's the world we live in, and it's probably similar to your world, too.

....

The following chapters will help you avoid mistakes commonly made by landowners. If you follow the lessons of this book, you will be successful, but in half the time it took us.

....

Thousands of people have visited our outdoors classroom, but we realize not everyone can visit the Demo Center. This book is designed to bring the Demo Center to our readers. A tour through the habitat-development Demo Center lasts about four hours and includes stops at about 20 sites, each illustrating a unique habitat-development concept. This book is organized along the same lines. Each chapter is set in one of our habitat-demo areas, and we encourage you to mentally place yourselves on our demo tour. In essence, this book is a "virtual" tour of NorthCountry Whitetails' Demo Center. Each chapter places you in an outdoor environment where you will learn a new aspect of habitat development and/or quality deer hunting.

Craig and Neil Dougherty with Craig's 150-plus buck taken on the NorthCountry Whitetails' Demo Center in 2002. Ten years before, bucks like this one were only a dream for the father-son team.

This Book: The Demo Center and More

When we started our habitat project, no books like this were available. We read some academic, research-oriented textbooks, but few dealt with habitat development, especially in the North. Our mentors helped chart our way and kept us from making too many big mistakes. Our property didn't come with a handbook or owner's manual. We made mistakes, as everyone does, but we learned from all of them. We hope the following chapters help you avoid common mistakes made by landowners in the early stages of their habitat-development journey. We hope the chapters motivate you, as well. We hope to start you on the path, or perhaps accelerate your progress, by sharing our knowledge and experience. We learned from our mentors, our endless research, and plenty of trial and error. Habitat development is not rocket science, but even today, few "hands-on" materials exist in printed form. If you follow the lessons of this book, you too will be successful - but in half the time it took us.

This is the second edition of Grow 'Em Right. The first edition was published three years earlier and has been a huge success. In fact, it is commonly viewed as the "Bible" of small (under 1,000 acres) deer hunting property management. Things have been moving extremely fast in the food plot and habitat development industry. Our knowledge as well as that of our readers has grown dramatically. While our first edition is still "dead on" in spirit, tone, and management concepts it contains some technical information that frankly, is dated. Every chapter of the first edition has been edited to reflect these changes in knowledge and information. We have eliminated old information and replaced it with the most current information we have at our disposal. In addition, we have added three chapters to the first edition in order to present a number of advanced concepts Neil and Craig have developed over the past three years. We are pleased to be able to offer our readers a second edition that will not only answer their questions, but take them to the next level of management as well.

Since starting the Demo Center tours, we have been thrilled with the public's response. Most of our "graduates" left the Demo Center feeling motivated, and have undertaken habitat-management programs of their own. They call and e-mail us year-round with questions and success stories. Virtually everyone who tours our property can relate it to his or her own property. The Whitetail Alliance short courses and special programs have also been a huge success.

We are confident this book will reach you in a similar way. We want you to envision yourself, your buddies, and your property in the pages ahead.

We hope you carry this book in your backpack or on the dashboard of your pickup truck; keep it handy for reference. Consult it often, and get copies for your friends and neighbors. It's a book to be used repeatedly. Put the first edition on the shelf as a memento of good times past. Follow the second edition closely, and your dream of creating quality deer hunting property will become a reality.

While Neil's trophy whitetail was a defining moment in our habitat-development journey, it was not the most important moment, that moment came in about 1990 when we decided to do something about the mediocre deer hunting we had long experienced. We decided to take matters into our own hands and change our hunting success. We hope this book helps create that moment for you.

So, dust off your imagination and jump on the tram. The tour is beginning.

Chapter II

Getting Started...
Make a Commitment,
Develop a Plan

Imagine the NorthCountry tram pulling into a small food plot. You get off and walk until you're standing by a tired old apple tree. Its top branches are severely pruned, and its limbs droop under the weight of bite-size apples. Deer tracks and droppings litter the ground. You notice a buck rub and scrape a few yards away. Hanging from one branch is a frayed yellow nylon rope.

Twelve years before, this tree had lain on the ground, the victim of a spring ice storm. The rope had been used to haul, hoist and secure the tree into an upright position.

This tree and its rope are symbols of our commitment to creating quality wildlife habitat. Most people would have left the tree on its side. For us, raising it was a symbolic act. Two weeks earlier, we have "released" the stressed apple tree from the grips of crowding brush, competing trees and a dense overstory. The work we did that day with a chainsaw was exhausting but rewarding. We saved the apple tree

Can you locate the deer in this photo? Thick cover like this provides food and cover for whitetails. Creating dense cover is relatively easy as long as "stemmy" material or wooded areas already exist. If you are working primarily with open spaces like fields, planting is the answer, but it takes more time and money.

from a slow, certain death. It hadn't borne fruit in years, but we went to sleep that night dreaming of deer feasting on its future bounty.

That had been our first habitat project, so we were crestfallen when we visited the property after the ice storm and saw the apple tree on its side. Righting toppled trees is not a practice we recommend, but on that early-spring day, the job needed to be done. After all, we had committed ourselves to creating quality wildlife habitat. Turning this tree into an apple-producing food source was part of our plan. We were determined to succeed.

Make a Commitment

You can't create a whitetail paradise without making a serious commitment. It just won't happen. The commitment requires both money and time. How much? That depends. Some properties require more time than money others require more money than time. At a minimum, on the money side you'll need basic tools such as chainsaws and pruning shears ($500). More likely, you'll also need food-plot implements such as tractors, plows, disks and ATVs (add $5,000). Further, high-quality seed is a must, as is lime and fertilizer ($100 or so per acre).

On the time side, you can mechanically prepare a seedbed, add fertilizer and lime and plant seed in about one half day per acre (provided nothing goes wrong). This assumes the food plot site has already been cleared and previously worked. Cutting brush and thinning trees, etc. Well lets just say "How much time do you have?" Lets just say you won't be playing much golf or going fishing while you are actively developing your property.

Oh yes, you'll also need knowledge. You need to know what projects need doing. How to do the work and how much time and money will be required. But that's why you are reading this book.

Creating food plots is part of most habitat-development programs. Food plots planted in high-quality forages create tons of highly nutritious forage for whitetails. This 1-acre food plot will be used by a dozen or so deer each day and even more each night.

Most habitat enthusiasts are do-it-yourselfers. In fact, many are weekend warriors with no more than a dozen workdays per year and limited budgets to spend on habitat projects. But take heart, you will get it done and you will experience a level of satisfaction second to none as your property begins to take shape. Your hunts will take on more meaning and you will experience a thrill like none other when you harvest your first mature buck from a food plot or

••

Are you a quick-fix person? If so, habitat development might not be for you. But if you're patient and want to be a good steward of the land — and you enjoy hunting and viewing quality game animals — you will likely get hooked on habitat development and what we call "quality deer hunting".

••

browse area you helped to create. But it's not all about killing. Nothing is more satisfying than seeing a half-dozen quality animals using a food plot you cleared and planted yourself. We did most of the work on the Demo Center, and we would not trade the thousands of hours we spent together for anything. Doing the work yourself and with friends or relatives brings you closer to the land and the people you care about.

Habitat development does not happen overnight. The work you do today might not benefit wildlife for months or even years. Yet we are confident every practice in this book will benefit wildlife, if implemented correctly. Are you a quick-fix person? If so, habitat development might not be for you. But if you're patient and want to be a good steward of the land – and you enjoy hunting and viewing quality game animals – you will likely get hooked on habitat development and what we call "quality deer hunting". Once that hook is set, few of us escape. Habitat development is contagious and self-perpetuating.

Let's discuss how to get started.

Finding Land to Buy

First, you need land with which to work. The most attractive option is to own the property where you'll be working. Ownership eliminates the hassles of landlords, lease arrangements, gaining and maintaining access, and so on. It allows you to do what you want with your land, and when you want to do it. The most common question asked in Neil's seminars is this: "How many acres do you need to improve the quality of your hunting?" His answer: "How many do you have?" We believe you can always improve your hunting through habitat development. You might not be able to manage a big herd (most experts say about 1,000 acres is required to truly manage deer), but you can change things for the better. Most landowners we work with own between 60 and 600 acres.

Of course, ownership is expensive, with good hunting land usually starting at a minimum of $2,000 per acre. Not only that, but good property is difficult to find. Although land prices might appear prohibitive, it helps to be creative when considering a purchase.

Recreational property often contains valuable timber that could – and often should – be cut. Harvesting timber is a great way to offset the cost of a land purchase. We once bought a beautiful 100-acre chunk of woods and paid for the entire property with a timber harvest. The timber needed cutting and we never missed it. In fact it could have been cut harder.

Land set asides, CRP programs, and forestry incentives can also be used to offset purchase price costs. Some enterprising landowners have made great deals selling "development rights" to conservation organizations, towns or other government municipalities. Basically the rights to build housing projects or strip malls or whatever are sold to an organization which wants to keep the property in an undeveloped state. I know a number of landowners who have cut the purchase price of their property in half or more by selling rights that they didn't want anyway. They own the property and can do anything with it except develop it. This of course affects resale value but if you didn't buy the property as an investment who cares?

Most of us need the help of some sort of mortgage in order to purchase a piece of property. Don't be discouraged when your bank turns you down. Most banks don't like to lend money on undeveloped land. If they do, they might want a down payment of 25-30%. This can be a pretty steep chunk of cash to come up with at today's land prices (which by the way are steadily climbing). Home equity loans are pretty effective when coming up with down payments and the interest on them is deductible.

Many landowners are willing to "hold the paper" on a property, because bank financing for undeveloped land can be difficult to obtain. You can often get by with 5%-10% down and low interest (say 2% over prime) when the seller becomes the bank. Landowners will often accept a low down payment if you agree to a large "balloon" payment in 5 years or so. An existing landowner who is eager to get out from under the tax burden often can be easy to work with. Especially if you approach the deal in the right way. Sometimes you come out way ahead by meeting his asking price if he will work with you on the payment terms side. The $5,000 you might have saved by dickering with him can be made up in the first year of mortgage payments.

Bottom line: Owning land is the best way to go, but requires money. Creative financing is often the way to obtain exceptional properties with little or no cash. It's not always easy, but if you can pull it off, you just might have landed the property of your dreams.

Be wary of group purchases. Best friends today are often sworn enemies tomorrow, especially when money is involved. Try to purchase property alone or with as few people as possible. Hunting camps are notorious for breaking up because of financial disputes, especially when second and third generation owners are involved. One owner, one set of rules. Everybody gets along.

Leasing: A Good Second Choice

Most hunters wrongly believe they must own land to improve their hunting through habitat development. This is especially true in some Northern areas where leasing is seldom practiced. Ownership is ideal, but not mandatory. Leasing is a realistic option. More and more property owners are interested in offsetting costs by granting access to hunters for a fee, and they're willing to allow those leasing property to do habitat projects.

....

If you lease property, be sure to have a legal agreement with a stipulated length and strong renewal language. This ensures work you do today benefits others tomorrow.

....

Lease costs vary, depending on the geographic area and the lease's quality. In our area of Steuben County, New York, leases can be had for as little as $5 - $10 per acre. When we wrote the first edition of this book three years ago the number was $3-$5. Other areas can cost as much as $20 per acre or more. In most areas of the country, leasing popularity is on the increase and costs are headed in the same direction.

If you lease property, be sure to have a legal agreement with a stipulated length and strong renewal language. This ensures the work you do today doesn't wind up benefiting others tomorrow.

Although it's best to have your lease drawn up by a lawyer, be sure it's written in easy-to-read language. "Lawyer-speak" can spook the landowner and dash all hopes of an agreement. It's also wise to ask your lawyer to include an "option-to-buy" and/or a "first-right-of-refusal" clause in the contract. By doing so, you won't be helpless if the landowner decides to sell the land you've been working on and investing in. In fact, a first-right-of refusal clause can keep a property from going on the market at all; keeping all sales conversations between you and the landowner.

Hunting By Permission: Be Careful

Another option, although not nearly as attractive as owning or leasing, is hunting by permission. "Permission hunting" is fading fast as private properties are becoming tied up in leases. However, some landowners might grant verbal permission to hunt and perform habitat-management work if you approach them correctly.

The key to the "permission-granted" option, like leasing, is securing access for extended time periods before investing time and money in the property. Try to be sure the friendly landowners will be there

Good farmer/hunter relations often result in permission to hunt. But be careful. Access permission is often a temporary condition, and it is difficult to manage habitat with only a "permission-to-hunt" agreement. Leases are far better. Land ownership is better yet.

for the long run. You do not want to invest time and money in food plots and other projects, and then lose access privileges in the future because someone came along and leased it out from under you.

Our 500 acres at the NorthCountry Habitat Demo Center started as a 150-acre acquisition. Next, we added a lease of 250 acres. Five years later we converted the lease into a purchase because of the option-to-buy clause in our lease. We completed our third purchase, of 100 acres, soon after. Acquiring hunting property in a piecemeal fashion is not unusual. Seldom do you find one piece of ground that is ideal for all purposes. Most hunters want or need more. Typically, hunting landowners start with one tract and add others as opportunity and money allow.

Start With a Site Evaluation and Wildlife Management Plan

Once you have secured property to work with, it's time to develop a wildlife managment plan. Begin with a site evaluation,

A habitat-development professional will conduct a site evaluation and write a management plan tailored to your goals, objectives and the site itself. Pros can save you time and money, but be active in the planning and implementation. The more a landowner stays involved with planning, the higher the success rate and deeper the satisfaction.

which is best conducted by a habitat-development specialist with an in-depth understanding of deer behavior and deer hunting. NorthCountry Whitetails produces dozens of management plans each year. Recommendations vary depending on the property and the client's goals and objectives.

Dave and Beth Buckley did our initial evaluation years ago. They visited the property and walked the entire acreage, examining its food sources, cover, access, security, boundaries and topography. They drafted specific recommendations and helped answer our implementation questions. They saved us time and money, and contributed greatly to our early success.

Evaluating Food

Let's review what to look for during a site evaluation. Existing food sources are a critical focus of any evaluation. Volumes have been written on the whitetail's preferred foods, so do some reading before you start evaluating your property's food sources. When evaluating food sources, look for signs of what whitetails are eating. Check brush and trees for nipped twigs, buds and grasses. Also look for potential food sources and possible food plot sites. Does the property have abandoned fields or tillable acres? Look for opportunities to drop trees and create new browse by encouraging regeneration. We call this a "browse-cut". Look at soil content and soil quality, especially moisture availability. Today's brush-choked field can be tomorrow's clover plot. It might just require a weekend of work.

In evaluating a site, you must take stock of what the deer are eating and what they don't touch. At the same time, identify opportunities to create food sources through "intervention".

Evaluating Cover

Cover is just as important as food. In fact, if your property is surrounded by abundant food sources or is in farm country, cover

This apple tree has been heavily browsed. In fact, it's unlikely to survive. Even though deer are fond of apple trees, browsing this severe indicates a food shortage. If additional overpopulation evidence is found, deer numbers must be reduced or food sources increased.

might be more important than food sources. Look for dense, brushy, impenetrable thickets that deer love to frequent. Remember, the deer's world exists from ground level to a height of about five feet. Above that, with the exception of mast-producing trees, little else matters to deer.

Whitetails – especially big bucks – crave a secure place to hang out. Dense cover is highly attractive to deer. Again, look at the property's potential as well as what already exists. A stand of four to six inch maple trees produces dense shade and doesn't allow anything to grow below. Deer find little reason to frequent in such stands. However, if you spend a day or two with a chainsaw, or better yet, a few hours with a bulldozer you can convert acres of pole timber into a productive browse-cut. This "green desert" of pole timber, with proper intervention, can be a home to the most reclusive white-tailed buck.

Creating cover is often the most important habitat-management practice you can employ. Neil worked on one such property a couple of years ago. The 170-acre property is long and narrow. About 30 percent of it is tillable, and another 30 percent is covered with uneven aged hardwood timber. The rest of the property features overgrown apple orchards with no ground cover, the result of dense shade from vines and climbing rose bushes. Deer passed through the property frequently and did some night feeding, but seldom hung around during daylight. The owners wanted to develop the property's daytime holding capability. Creating cover was the key, along with planting high-quality forage. A chainsaw crew spent a few weekends eliminating the orchards' overstory. The "fresh" sunlight allowed dense ground cover to re-emerge. A logging crew took care of the hardwood stand and provided some much needed cash for seed and fertilizer.

After the chainsaw work was completed. These areas were soon on their way to becoming secure holding cover. The owners then added a few strategically placed food plots to concentrate the deer on the property, thus completing the habitat turnaround.

This deer is enjoying the benefits of cover, which includes food and protection from predators and weather. In evaluating a property's suitability for whitetails, be sure to think about its cover potential.

Within two years, thanks to the cover that was created, the property became a holding property instead of a pass-through property. The owners were happy and so were the deer.

Evaluate Access

Access is the third major factor in evaluating property. Hunting properties must be accessible in order to realize their recreational potential. A network of trails and roads is important for managing a property. Access roads allow equipment to be moved from place to place to work on projects.

The NorthCountry Demo Center took a huge step forward when we created a truck-friendly access road to connect both ends of the property. This road allowed commercial lime and fertilizer trucks to reach almost all of our food plots, cutting labor and material

A network of access roads is important to a managed property. Roads and trails not only provide hunting access, but they enable you to move equipment in and out of areas needing attention. "Forever wild" is a nice concept to read about, but if you want quality habitat, you need a network of roads to get some work done.

costs dramatically. This access road is bordered by high-quality clover, and is often used by deer, turkeys and bears. It produces miles of ultra-attractive edge environment. The bulldozer work required to construct the road was significant, and at times ugly, but the outcome was worth it.

Not all access roads need to accommodate heavy equipment. Others can be ATV trails that allow you to get in and out of your property with little disturbance to wildlife. The same holds true for walking trails, which are equally important. When evaluating a property, look closely at access. Whitetails adapt to human activity on access roads, and are seldom panicked when we approach. Restricting your movement to access roads allows access and won't push wildlife from you property.

You cannot manage a property without managing trespassing. Pay attention to this aspect of ownership when considering a property for lease or purchase. If you already own or lease hunting land, concentrate on eliminating all trespassing. Posting parties get the job done.

Evaluate Unwanted Access

Unfortunately, unwanted access must also be considered, especially in populated areas. Trespassing is a fact of life and not all "visitors" are desirable. When evaluating a property for purchase or lease, pay attention to the neighborhood. You wouldn't buy a home in the middle of a high-crime neighborhood. The same holds true for hunting land. Learn how many neighbors border the property and who they are. If known poachers and troublemakers are abundant, perhaps you

should look elsewhere. Outlaws can make life miserable. Also look at roads that intersect the property. If your 100-acre paradise is chopped up by two or three public roads, it could be a security nightmare. Always look for properties that discourage access by unwanted visitors.

If you already own a "high-maintenance" property, you have no choice but to deal with it. It's never too late to implement a no-tres-passing policy. This requires that you prosecute trespassers and aggressively post your property against trespassing. When looking at property, it's easy to disregard the trespassing issue. Don't! Each year, Neil answers hundreds of questions about trespassing from people at his shows and seminars. Trespass problems are one of his hottest topics. The issue is real, and you must address it early in your planning.

Management Plan: Goals, Practices, Budgets and Timelines

After evaluating a property, it is important to establish goals for the land. This is an important step, and the help of a specialist pays huge dividends. Not all landowners have the same objectives. Some want to grow trophy deer while others prefer to see an abun-dance of wildlife. Many want both. Once you set your goals, you must develop a plan to achieve them. The plan should outline habi-tat-development activities, including time and cost in order of pri-ority, and the ease of successful completion. Early in the develop-ment of our NorthCountry facility, we identified dozens of wild apple trees in stressed, overcrowded conditions, including the ones at the beginning of this chapter. They were in decline and seemed destined to be firewood. It was important to "release" them, that is, remove competing trees and brush.

We also needed to prune them to reverse the decline. This was not only a useful and logical first step, but it was also financially feasible for a start-up operation. It required only a chainsaw, prun-ing shears, safety gear, and a few pounds of fertilizer. Best of all,

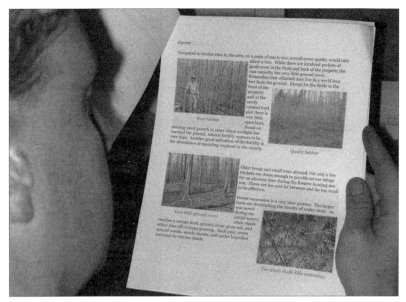

Most plans developed by NorthCountry Whitetails typically include an aerial photo of the property complete with food plots, sanctuaries, and access trails and roads located. The aerial photo serves as a map and working blueprint for the property. Background information is also included with the plan.

we finished the work with a feeling of accomplishment and optimism. We saw tangible results immediately when deer browsed the pruned limbs, and soon after we saw strong regrowth during spring and summer. A ruffed grouse hatched a brood under a pile of pruned limbs the first spring after the work was completed.

Your plan should contain a clear statement of goals, a set of strategies to achieve the goals, a list of practices you intend to undertake, a realistic timeline (stated in man hours of work, not just months on a calendar) and an equally realistic budget in dollars and cents.

Set Priorities for Success

When identifying projects, be sure they are "doable" within your time and expense boundaries. Nothing is more discouraging to beginning land-mangers than tackling a project that never ends or gets too expensive. Accomplishing a series of small projects is more rewarding and beneficial to wildlife than starting many and completing few, if any. Do the easy stuff first. Take small steps and, if possible, work with a habitat-development specialist to avoid unnecessary mistakes that cost time and money.

Be sure to put your plan in writing, even if it's just an outline. Committing your goals and priorities to writing not only sharpens your thinking, but also provides motivation. You don't have to cast your plan in concrete, but you'll find it helpful to commit it to writing.

Be sure to share your plan with the people necessary to get you there. Your family needs to "buy into" the plan not only in dollars and sense but in time commitment as well. If you plan on help from your hunting buddies they should also be in on the planning. They need to know what you are counting on them to do and when you need them.

One final note on planning. Plan to have fun. You can get so wrapped up in this stuff that it becomes all work and no fun. A nev- erending task to be accomplished. This can be really tough on the family. Especially the kids. Build in playtime or at least schedule some down time. You will get more accomplished in the long haul.

As you read through the rest of this book start thinking about developing your plan; you might even make an outline as you go. Jot down ideas as you read. Write in the margins. When you fin- ish your first reading take a stab at your first management plan. You'll have a blast doing it and it will help you master the ideas presented in the book. Read and revise, then read and revise again. Go ahead and give us a call if you are stuck. That's why we are here. Need Neil to come out for a visit? He does dozens of wildlife management plans each year. Above all; enjoy.

Chapter III

A Chainsaw is a Deer's Best Friend

Imagine you have just entered a one-acre, irregular-shaped clearing. The area contains five mature apple trees and three five-year-old apple saplings, all of which are surrounded by brush piles that protect them from browsing deer. The ground is covered with brambles, berry bushes and grasses, especially inside the skeletal remains of trees felled seven years before. Deer trails, droppings and rubs abound. A ladder stand is strategically placed near the intersection of three trails. This place looks and feels like a deer hangout, but it was not always so. Eight years ago, it was canopied by sun-shielding pole timber. Nothing grew at deer level. There was no food and cover; just dirt and a few leaves strewn under the dense pole timber.

We call this place "Wayne's World", because it was a favorite hunting spot of our friend Wayne. Three decades earlier, this 20-acre section of side hill was an eroding sheep pasture with a southern expo-

Photo by Charles J. Alsheimer

Does hang near cover for food and safety. This buck jumped this doe in thick cover. Does also use dense cover to hide from aggressive bucks. This doe has been driven into the open by the big guy.

sure. Fifteen years of successional growth resulted in dense brush, which gave way to a canopy of pole timber years later. A small stand of wind-deflecting pines bordered the clearing to the west. Overgrown apple trees and an occasional hardwood completed the habitat mosaic. For the first two to three years we owned our property, deer seemed to just hang out at Wayne's World. The hunting was super. But over time, we noticed the deer stopped frequenting this location. Even Wayne, who christened it his favorite place to hunt, began to hunt other locations. The hotspot grew cold, but why?

One afternoon in June, the answer came to us as we stood in Wayne's World. It was dark. Not night dark; just heavy, dense, canopied woods dark. A dense overstory of vegetation was thriving 20 to 30 feet above us, but nothing was growing on the ground. No wonder there were no deer. This was 2 o'clock in the afternoon, and no sunlight was reaching the ground. It was time - past time, in fact - to take action.

The next winter, four men with chainsaws, safety gear, an ax and a few wedges were again in the spot. In 16 hours of work, we created a relatively open half-acre clearing, leaving only a few mature trees standing. We piled the brush cuttings to strategically direct deer movements. We cut it aggressively, cutting all the poles to ground level. We planted a few apple trees to complement the old-timers, and stacked brush around them for protection from browsing deer, but other than that, we left the site alone.

Today, briars and berry bushes grow everywhere. The apple trees are producing fruit, and deer sign is abundant. In just three short years, Wayne's World is once again a hotspot.

This scenario illustrates how the dynamic properties of nature are ever changing, and can sneak up on you. Twelve years before, Wayne's World was a hotspot

Photo by Charles J. Alsheimer

Browse is vital to deer and relatively easy to create. No matter how many crops are available, deer still need, and eat, lots of browse. A dense opening like this spot is a "bed-and-breakfast" stop for this big fellow.

where deer hung out. Three years later, the same location was a dead zone for deer. The only deer we saw were on their way to other areas. Our chainsaw intervention transformed an area devoid of deer into a popular staging area and a favorite hunting spot once more.

Chainsaws Create Food

Motivated by the results at Wayne's World, we have since spent countless hours investigating the feeding habits of deer, and creating browse at the NorthCountry Demo Center. It's important to understand that most of a deer's food exists within six feet of the ground. Deer feed on forbs, leaves, grasses and browse stems. Hard masts like acorns are also a favorite, as are soft masts like apples, lichens and mushrooms. The first 1 to 3 inches of new growth on a branch or twig provides the best browse; the first inch provides most of the protein the farther down the stem the deer eats the poorer the food quality. Stemmy browse contains a high percentage of hard to digest lignin; it is of little benefit to deer. The average protein content of red maple browse on our facility is 5 percent to 6 percent.

When limbs within reach of deer are repeatedly browsed off, trees shift their growth energy elsewhere, and the new growth sprouts above the deer's reach. The food source disappears or worse, dies. To see this condition in the extreme, examine woodlots where livestock have fed. Virtually nothing is left at ground level. When you see conditions like this in the woods, you have

Deer have browsed more than one inch from these shoots. This is not a good sign. It indicates a food shortage for deer in this area. You have two choices: create more food or reduce deer numbers. A combination of the two will probably work best.

This twig is lightly browsed, less than an inch from its tip has been eaten. The deer that nipped this twig got maximum nutrition for minimal effort. This is a sign that deer numbers and available food are likely in sync, assuming this is a preferred browse species.

real herd management problems: too many deer, too little food. Natural regenerating brambles and young tree stems are all very good food sources, but they grown at ground level and require lots of sunlight to prosper. Sunlight is the key, but an over abundance of deer can eliminate browse in even the sunniest areas.

You can keep track of browse impact on your own property by erecting a browse exclosure in the woods. Fence off (6ft. high) a 25ft.x25ft. section of woods that has recently been opened up. Be sure the area around it is in the same condition. Deer will browse around it but the inside will be untouched. If your deer density is high in a matter of months you will begin to see the difference. In a matter of years the cage will be thick with brush while the areas outside of the cage remain "brush bare". If your deer numbers are "under control" the outside and inside of the cage will not be dramatically different from the inside.

Site the cage where all your hunters can see it. This will make them aware of the impact deer make on native habitat and can get reluctant doe shooters to get with the doe harvest program.

We recently undertook a study with Charlie Alsheimer in which he placed cuttings from assorted browse species into one of his deer-research enclosures. We were interested not only in what the deer preferred to browse, but the protein content of each browse species. Charlie documented the browse in order of the deer's preference from greatest to least, but when the protein results came

Highly Preferred Species in Order of Preference Percentages represent crude protein and crude fiber respectively.			
Species	**May 15, 2001**	**Aug. 15, 2001**	**Dec. 15, 2001**
1. Wild Apple	3.8% - 5.6%	11.7% - 12.3%	4.2% - 19.7%
2. Basswood	6.1% - 4.3%	6.9% - 7.4%	3.4% - 20.2%
3. Ash	4.8% - 6.7%	6.7% - 11.4%	3.3% - 30.7%
4. Aspen	9.1% - 12.9%	6.1% - 9.3%	5.1% - 17.6%
5. Hard Maple	7.0% - 8.8%	4.8% - 9.8%	4.6% - 25.7%
6. Red Oak	5.6% - 7.5%	6.8% - 11.3%	3.0% - 31.7%
7. Staghorn Sumac	6.3% - 4.1%	7.5% - 4.0%	6.0% - 28.0%
8. Raspberry plants	5.0% - 5.4%	N/A	N/A
9. Black Cherry	13.4% -12.8%	5.9% - 7.1%	3.2% - 18.2%
10. Wild Strawberry	3.1% - 4.1%	N/A	N/A
Non-preferred Species - Eaten If Other Browse is Unavailable			
11. American Beech	7.4% - 12.7%	7.8% - 13.2%	4.3% - 23.6%
12. Striped Maple	9.8% - 8.6%	2.5% - 3.5%	2.4% - 20.4%
Highly Preferred Winter Food*			
1. White Cedar	N/A	N/A	4.2% - 12.7%
2. Hemlock	N/A	N/A	3.6% - 11.2%

* White cedar and hemlock are highly preferred by Charlie Alsheimer's enclosure deer and by wild deer during winter. Their preference for these two types of browse at this time of year rivals their preference for the top four preferred foods on the above list. However, white cedar and hemlock are not browsed much, if at all, during the rest of the year.

back from the NEAS Diagnostic Laboratory of Cornell University, we were surprised. The deer did not consistently gravitate to high-protein food, as has been frequently stated in print. Their preferences changed with the time of year.

Because Charlie is familiar with the deer in this study, he could also note individual preferences. Deer, like humans, seem to prefer certain foods. Instance, one of Charlie's bucks loves to eat American beech browse, while the other deer in the enclosure seldom, if ever, browse beech. Charlie also has a doe that loves aspen and always chooses it over other foods.

A lot can be learned about deer from observing their feeding behavior, and an astute observer can learn a lot about his property by analyzing those feeding behaviors, especially if he observes it year-round. You don't need to be an expert to observe which food sources deer use on your property. Don't be surprised if they don't fall in line with what the experts report.

In other words, don't accept everything you read about deer behavior as absolute truth. Sharp eyes and an inquisitive mind reveal much. Always, always observe and analyze the deer behavior you observe on your property; especially when it comes to feeding behavior.

Browse as a Population Index

Evaluating browse use helps estimate the amount of deer food available in an area. Look at a plant and see if the 1-inch tips are browsed off or if 3 or 4 inches of stem or twig are torn away. The entire stem might be consumed by deer during a severe winter. If you find gross browse consumption, you need fewer deer and/or better food sources. Increasing the amount of deer browse helps correct the problem. When you produce enough browse tonnage, and other sources of nourishment such as food plots, your deer will begin to use just the tips of the stems. You need to get to where they eat only the last inch or half-inch.

Growing season browsing is often an indication of too many deer or not enough low lignin food sources like clover and chicory. Planting more food plots and or logging roads will often correct this problem.

The best time to evaluate browse impact is at the end of the growing season. Woody plants browsed during growing season typically dry rot down the stem from where they were nipped. The more time expires after the browsing event the more stem rot is in evidence. Nipped stems dry rot at the following rate: ¼"-30 days, ½"-45 days, 1"- 60 days. Use this scale to determine when a stem was nipped. If you find heavy mid summer (drought free) browsing you should be concerned as deer normally are light browsers during mid summer.

Reducing the number of deer on your property is another strategy to keep a constant supply of quality deer browse available. Many wooded areas have so many deer that they all but eliminate forest regeneration. This is a serious problem not only for the deer but for forested areas as well.

This aggressive clearcut at our facility covers about 5 acres and runs through the center of a beautiful stand of oaks. In two to three years it will be "prime real estate," providing a travel corridor throughout the woods as well as a "bed and breakfast" among the relatively open oak timber. Talk about structure!

White-tailed deer, and most wildlife, for that matter, thrive in dense cover conditions. Now that Wayne's World has been restored to excellent deer habitat, guests on our tours see the contrast with an adjoining woodlot, which we left uncut for demonstration purposes. At "deer level", you see a dense stand of hardwood pole timber up to 12 inches in diameter, and nothing else. The crowns have grown together, preventing most of the sunlight from reaching the forest floor. Little food or cover is available. This is prime "people habitat", but deer do not spend time in this wide-open woodlot. They prefer the thick ground cover of Wayne's World.

Chainsaws Create Cover

Wildlife habitat should be thick enough to make it difficult for people to walk through, and almost impossible to sneak through. Brambles and underbrush hide deer and make noise when people

Photo by Charles J. Alsheimer

This buck is secure in this dense cover. His food is within steps of his bed. It is impossible for a hunter to approach quietly, so he can disappear long before a noisy human can get within his danger zone. This is quality deer habitat!

move through, alerting deer to slip out the backside unseen. Concealing cover can be anything from timbered treetops or underbrush near a small rise or ridge, to a dense stand of pines or spruce. A quick escape route helps deer feel comfortable in these areas. The more cover the better. Deer prefer to stay within 60 yards of dense cover so they can disappear in two to three seconds.

Deer, like fish; are drawn to structure. The fish structure analogy is helpful when thinking about deer. If you have a wide-open, one-dimensional forest or woodlot, you must drop trees and create structure. Plants will grow where daylight reaches the ground, producing different levels of growth and cover. Another fish analogy is that big fish prefer structure, in part, because it attracts smaller fish (food and bait). Deer also need cover and food, so they are attracted to structure in their habitat. In the case of big bucks, the does that frequent the structure are bait. When creating structure, first consider areas around natural or existing food sources, such as apple trees or clusters of oaks. Structure in conjunction with food is a tough combination to beat.

Try to create little pockets of cover 50 to 60 yards across throughout your property. Arrange them along known buck travel routes. These areas of structure will attract does, creating a prime environment for hunting for bucks. During the pre-rut and rut, bucks will go from structure to structure searching for that doe in heat. The goal in these small cuts, which cover up to 1 acre or so is to maximize food diversity and create cover. If laid out correctly, it will help you pattern bucks as they move from doe hole to doe hole.

Plan Before You Cut

Chainsaw work can also help control deer movement. Strategically cutting and placing felled trees manipulates how deer travel through the property. The goal is to create predictable deer movements. Trees left on the ground can guide deer movements through certain locations, allowing you to beat the whitetail's nose and set up a high-percentage downwind ambush.

This timber has been leveled, leaving plenty of room for sunlight to reach the ground and "inspire" vegetation. Brush will be piled strategically to alter deer movements and protect young trees from being browsed. Dense spruce will also be planted in strategic areas. This area will be a deer hot spot for about the next 10 years.

Aggressive cutting creates what we call "browse-cuts". These are akin to clearcuts, but because clearcuts have developed a bad name, we prefer to call them browse-cuts. Browse-cuts are also usually smaller than clearcuts, which got their bad name because they often cover hundreds of acres, and create large disturbances to the terrain.

It is difficult to remove too many trees in a browse-cut. More often than not, landowners are too conservative with the saw, and leave too many trees, which shade the ground after a year or two growth. We drop almost all the trees in the cut, from 18 to 20 inches down to 2 inches in diameter. We convert mature trees into saw logs and sell them. We cut smaller pieces for firewood, but we always leave some in the woods, especially treetops. It might be more important to get structure into the area than to harvest every stick of firewood. Leaving treetops in the cutting area is the quickest way to create ground structure. Try not to leave tops more than 4 feet in the air. That way, deer can browse the tender tips, especially if you are sawing in winter, which is the preferred time to cut. Tops kept close to the ground will also create a better-looking woodlot.

Create Living Brush Piles

We create living brush piles by dropping small trees or shrubs without cutting them clear through. We do this by felling small trees with a cut that doesn't sever it from the stump. The tree will lie on the ground and remain alive for perhaps a few years, providing thick cover and nutritious browse. Shrubs and small trees in the three to six inch range respond better to this treatment than do large ones. This maximizes the amount of food tonnage, and provides cover for other wildlife. You can also push over small trees with a bulldozer or tractor to create living brush piles. These will live even longer.

Unfortunately, trees treated this way are not always a thing of beauty. In fact, some woods purists prefer a "total cut or none at all" approach; arguing the tree deserves as much. Some day we may become sensitized to that degree but at present we are content with an end justifies the means approach to habitat creation.

Leave Tree Tops on the Ground

The work done in Wayne's World is an excellent example of a browse-cut. This area was enhanced by planting several young apple trees and "releasing" several old and overgrown ones. We "released" them by removing the overstory and surrounding brush that competed for moisture and soil nutrients, and then pruned their spindly limbs, and fertilized the root system to increase apple production. We protected the young plantings from becoming deer snacks by piling brush in a 6-foot diameter around the sapling, 2 or 3 feet high. These treetops produced a "cage" that prevented deer from eating the young "whips".

This tipped-over tree will live on its side for a few years, providing dense cover and food for deer. For a living brush pile, push pole timber over with a tractor bucket or bulldozer, or cut them most of the way through and let them settle to the ground.

Tops on the ground provide a caging effect that allows native tree species to regenerate. Deer choose not to walk through the downed tree tops because of their density. This reduces browsing dramatically. The spaces between limbs become protected nurseries for regenerating trees and shrubs.

Treetops and limbs can also be stacked to create habitat for all kinds of critters. Build your wildlife brush pile by putting the largest logs on the bottom and stacking brush to about 6-feet high. This setup attracts rabbits and other small game.

The most effective way to lay out a browse-cut and create structure is to make a series of quarter to half-acre cuts in a wooded area, felling most of the trees. Drop all the trees into a few strategically chosen target areas, creating small, dense structures. The area under the tops will regenerate tree growth, while the unprotected area should produce knee-high ground growth around the outer fringe. Another approach is to cut long "power lines" through the woods, which will become browse and travel corridors. Mature bucks will generally travel slightly downwind of these types of cuts in order to keep track of the does using the cuts.

Cut Strategically, but be Aggressive

Good wildlife habitat should look nasty. Removing 70% of tree stems in an area is generally necessary for good browse to thrive. You might even be embarrassed to show people the cutting for a couple of years, because of its appearance, but gradually it will begin to look like prime whitetail habitat. At the NorthCountry Demo Center, we show before and after browse-cut areas. This helps visitors gain the confidence to aggressively cut for browse and cover. Don't be alarmed when you create habitat. In addition to high-quality food plots, we want native species to regenerate, and this will occur only if you put light on the ground. At the Demo Center, we are constantly setting back Mother Nature's natural succession. Deer feel more secure in these environments.

Crush Your Brush

Over the past three years we have been relying heavily on bulldozer work to create habitat. We call it "crush your brush" and it works fantastically. Basically you fire up a decent sized dozer, raise the blade 2 to 3 feet off the ground and drive over whatever brush and pole size timber might get in your way. It works beautifully, but boy is it ugly. Pole sized timber is barked up, partially uprooted and lain on its side. Existing brush is crushed and left as wadded up piles of cover. You can turn an acre of ground into an impossible to penetrate (at least by humans) mess in an hour or so.

The beauty is, wildlife love it. Deer are on it within hours, if not minutes. It is instant food and cover. The partially uprooted pole timber continues to grow on its side (generally for two to three years) before finally dying. Deer can browse tender new growth

This browse-cut is a "mess," but it's a beautiful mess from a deer's perspective. New shoots are already coming up, and by summer the place will be a mass of green. This area will be productive for about 15 years, and then out comes the chainsaw again.

along its entire length that often amounts to thirty or forty feet or more. By the time the tree does die new sprouts are generally off to a start, growing under the shelter of the tipped over tree. The crushed brush quickly sends up tender new sprouts as a result of a new invigorating supply of sunlight. This procedure even creates water as "watering holes" are often created in the craters created by the partially uprooted trees.

Native grasses, forbs and other such greenery thrive in these areas and within a couple of months they cover all or most of the ugly "scars" left by the dozer. The following year the scars are healed and the area is as pretty a picture as one could imagine and a wildlife hot spot. If the "mess" bothers you(some people hate mess in the woods) "hide" the dozer work by keeping the work back from known human travel corridors. This way the wildlife will get the benefit of the food and cover and humans can continue to enjoy their "people habitat".

We recently were paid a visit by a couple of National Wild Turkey Federation Biologists who did a TV program on our property. They absolutely fell in love with the turkey-nesting habitat created by the brush crushing. They pointed out that hundreds of "turkey tents" perfect for nesting were created as native grasses grew over the tops of the downed saplings. This coupled with adjoining food plots created ideal brood raising conditions.

Dozers are big bad beasts that can really do some damage. Be careful! Crushing brush can be extremely dangerous. Twisted and bent saplings store enormous energy and can "spring" at any time. They are capable of inflicting serious injury or worse. Loggers outfit their "woods dozers" with protective cages to keep flying debris, tree limbs and saplings out and operators in. Hire a professional operator or if you must do it yourself be sure to wear eye, ear and head protection, heavy steel toed boots, tough leather gloves and anything else you can think of to put between you and exploding tree parts. Most importantly use dozers with "caged in cabs" and yes buckle up before operating.

One further note on dozers; guys love to operate them and everyone wants one of their own. It's a power thing. If you are thinking about buying one forget it! We own two of the damn things and one of them is always broken (unless they are both broken). They are expensive to fix and always, always, break in the middle of an important job. Bottom line: the only ones that run are new ones, the only ones you can afford are old ones. Better rent than buy. But they sure look good sitting out there in your equipment barn. Wouldn't sell ours for nothing.

Wayne's World Revisited

Remember Wayne's story? The first time he walked in there after the browse-cut, he said: "What did you do? This place used to be beautiful. It looks like it was hit with a tornado."

We created 1½ acres of brush piles and downed trees. It's important to know what a browse-cut looks like. If you only cut to where you are aesthetically comfortable, you probably aren't cutting enough. Today, Wayne's World once again looks beautiful, especially to the deer that hang out there.

In hindsight, we should have been even more aggressive in cutting Wayne's World. We reached a point in our cutting and clearing where we believed we needed to leave some trees. Now they have grown, and they need to come down. The chainsaws must come out again. A successful browse-cut maximizes light. With trees 30 to 40 feet high, the entire food source is in the treetops. Plus, the tree's roots suck valuable nutrients from the soil that could be used by browse generating plants. As soon as you drop those trees, you establish cover and browse for the next year. In fertile areas, browse will spring up almost immediately.

The first year, you can expect existing stumps to send up shoots, and you will see occasional forbs, grasses, brambles, blackberries and raspberries. The second year will show a dramatic increase in woody stems, brambles and stump shoots. Typically, brambles begin taking over in the third year, to be followed in later years by larger and more aggressive woody stem development. If you have an environment with poor soil, regeneration can be enhanced with a dose of lime and/or fertilizer. This can accelerate regeneration by a couple of years.

Not only is the chainsaw a deer's best friend, it's a habitat manager's best friend, too. With an investment of about $500 for a quality saw, a pair of chaps, some steel toed boots and a safety helmet with ear and eye protection, you can do wonders for wildlife, especially white-tailed deer. With a chainsaw, you can do years of habitat development work without owning a tractor or building a food plot. It's usually the best way to begin improving your property.

Hack and Squirt

Some habitat managers prefer herbicide treatments to the chainsaw. Called "hack and squirt", you simply choose the tree, hack it with an ax or other cutting tool, squirt the cut with an herbicide. The tree starts to die shortly thereafter. It is reported to be highly effective and much less labor intensive than a chainsaw. We prefer the instant gratification of seeing the tree on the ground as the tops provide browse and cover and we are better able to shape the clearing.

Snipping and Sticking

We don't usually do a lot of tree and shrub planting but this technique is too simple to skip. Syracuse, NY landscape professional and horticulturalist Jim Sollecito has had great luck creating cover by "snipping and sticking" native brush species. The procedure is simple and works best on cane-like shrubs like dogwood, and shrub willows.

Jim takes a sharp pruning shears (cutting shears not the crushing anvil type) and snips pencil thick cuttings from dormant shrubs like

willow and dogwood. He collects 150 or so 12" shoots in a bucket and heads for an area that could use a "brush transplant". He shoves the lowest end of the cutting 2/3 of the way into the ground and moves on. Roots develop through the spring and before you know it your "stick" is a multi-stemmed shrub. According to Jim this is how the nursery people start the shrubs they sell to us for big bucks.

Our most recent cuts have been ultra aggressive. It looks barren now, but in no time this browse-cut will provide whitetails everything they need to survive. Planting the center road in clover will be a bonus.

Plant the entire bucket and by summer you will have a nice hefty patch of brush cover or perhaps a brush travel corridor. This is a great early spring or winter (thawed ground) practice that will put brush exactly where you need it most. Best of all it uses hardy native species and costs nothing.

PATROLLED
PRIVATE PROPERTY
All Persons Are Warned Against
Hunting, Fishing, Trapping Or
TRESPASSING
Hereon For Any Purpose
PENALTY $250.00
Posted in Accordance with the Provisions
of Section 366 of the Conservation Law
C & N DOUGHERTY
RD #7, BOX 166, FULTON, NY 13069

SANCTUARY
KEEP OUT

Chapter IV

Property Access:
Preventing and Creating

The NorthCountry tram turns down an access lane, which leads from a seldom-used public dirt road to a beautiful 40-acre stand of oaks. You stop in front of a cable gate that separates the public road from the lane. Three well-used deer trails cross the road within sight. Deer are crossing the public road at will. Up drives a run-down pickup truck with three scraggly passengers staring out. They are riding the roads a month before deer season, looking for "hunting" opportunities.

Deer sign is everywhere, but road hunters won't stop here. Displayed prominently is a plywood-backed yellow aluminum sign stating, "POSTED AND PATROLLED". The sign is just one of dozens displayed along the public road. The sign sends a strong message to would-be trespassers. The gate, which secures this right-of-way, sends another strong message against trespassing: Someone is serious about security on this property, judging by the gates and signs. It was not always this way, however. Twelve years before, this oak flat was "free range", and hunters from all over the area came and went. Only a few scattered signs were posted, and the landowner lived in California. Now, only invited guests dare enter this property.

Property access is about two things: making access easy for legitimate users and denying it to everyone else. Both are vital to managing habitat and quality deer hunting, but the issue of denying access arises most often in conversations with landowners.

Get the "No Trespassing" Message Out Quickly

One week after we bought the NorthCountry property, we were huddled around a July campfire when a truck came up the dirt road. It pulled over and we met our neighbor, Willis, for the first time. "So, you're the new owners," he said. "Going to Hunt?"

"Yes, we plan to hunt, and we'll post the property against trespassing," I said. "Good luck!" he said slowly. "This property has

....

Property access is about two things: making access easy for legitimate visitors and denying it to everyone else. Both are vital to managing habitat and quality deer hunting.

....

been open hunting for years, and a lot of people will still feel that way. They've always hunted here. People won't quit just because you say so. You'll have your hands full keeping them out. And if you try to …Oh well, you'll see."

Absentee landowners often have this problem. In fact, immediately after acquiring new land, you can expect to face trespassing problems, even if you live on the property. They will be short-lived, however, if you take the proper steps.

This "bulletproof" gate sends a no-nonsense message to would-be trespassers. It says, "These people are serious about their privacy and will take measures to preserve it." Simpler gates can be bought at most feed-and-seed stores for about $50.

Soon after our conversation with Willis, we began a security program on our property. We took obvious, deliberate steps to send the message that hunting without permission would not be allowed. First, we posted the land, next we contacted the sheriff and game warden, told them who we were and what we planned to do. We said we were posting the land, and asked them to help spread the word. Before long, locals knew the rules had changed on the "old McChesney place".

It was important to send the signal that we were reasonable people, but we insisted on ground rules. We let the locals know we might still grant permission to hunt or trespass, but we needed to know who was there and when and what they were doing. We insisted on a policy of hunting by written permission only. With this policy, you can be viewed as a good neighbor while gaining control of your property. It also allows you to meet many of the people who have already hunted your property. Then it's easy to sort out the "undesirables" from the "maybes". You can then begin

This cabled gate is covered with 3-inch PVC pipe. The white pipe is visible and less likely to cause accidents than hard-to-see steel cable. The posted sign in the middle adds the final touch. We used scrap material, but the new stuff costs less than $10.

to explain your hunting-management program, and tell them why it's not a good idea for them to hunt on your land. In other cases you might include them in "management deer" only hunts on specific days. You can also meet "contacts" that might help with your program. In our experience, aggressive posting discourages all but the most obnoxious trespassers.

Gate All Public-Road Access Lanes

Next, we gated all of our access lanes with a visible signal of ownership and restriction. For our main gate we chose an impressive welded-pipe structure that signaled, "Serious owners live here". We shut off most of our access roads with a cable threaded through two 6-foot pieces of 3-inch white PVC pipe for increased visibility and safety.

Gating and posting access roads is a must if you're to manage your property. You can't afford to have trespassers running deer from your property or harvesting deer without your knowledge. But controlling your property is also crucial for liability reasons. Just thinking about the safety implications of trespassers sneaking around while you or your friends are hunting should make you shudder. One accident could ruin a lifetime of hunting for you, your family and friends, and possibly destroy you financially.

This sign is an excellent example of how posting should be done. The sign is supported by a board backer. It has aggressive wording and it's highly visible. It cost about $2 per sign, but is well worth it in the long run.

Post Aggressively

Posting is usually done with some sort of signage. Signs are available in three types: paper, plastic or aluminum. States and municipalities have different laws; so check local regulations to ensure you post your property legally. It's no fun to have a trespasser beat you in court because of a technicality in posting regulations. But don't settle for the legal minimum when posting. You might have to post more aggressively than the law requires in order to be effective.

Paper signs are the least expensive, but require the most maintenance. You must walk the boundary and replace them every year. Plastic signs are much better, with most lasting about five years before fading, cracking and pulling out at the nails. Aluminum signs are the most durable, especially when paired with backer boards. This last option is more expensive, but wood-backed aluminum signs often stay on a tree 15 to 20 years. Custom-printed metal signs cost about $1.99 each. Pressure treated plywood backer boards cost about 50 cents and in the long run, they're much more cost effective.

The preferred method is to fasten the signs to boards before heading to the woods. Backer boards should be pressure-treated 3/8-inch plywood or 3/4-inch boards. Rough sawn scrap boards are excellent, but the necessary 11-inch width is difficult to find. You have to fasten a few together with cleats on the back to make a backer out of the narrower board. When posting, drive aluminum or galvanized nails through the board/sign and into the tree, leaving an inch of nail protruding to allow for tree growth. Center fasten the backed signs with two or three nails.

The backer boards and metal signs send a signal that you're serious about restricting access. Put yourself in a would-be trespasser's shoes. He is driving down the road and sees aluminum

Tired old signs like this are an invitation to trespassers. Perhaps the landowner has moved, but certainly he does not care enough about trespassing to keep his boundaries well-posted. Paper signs quickly turn old and must be regularly replaced.

signs with backer boards, clearly visible and closely spaced. Then he enters a stretch of road with old signs that are beat up and erratically spaced, perhaps hanging by one nail and difficult to see. If you were he, which property would you avoid and which would you poach on?

As a general guide, make sure potential trespassers cannot cross a property boundary without seeing a sign. In thick areas, you might place one every 30 yards, but you might get by spacing them 70 yards

- -

If legal, include the maximum trespassing fine on your signs. The law in our area sets the maximum fine at $250

- -

apart in more open areas, also, post signs often near pullovers on roads and in human travel corridors, such as draws, ridgetops and clearings. You can usually predict where a human will try to cross your line.

Certain states require that signs comply with legal specifications. Usually, signs must be of a certain size and include the landowner's name and a clear message against trespassing. When the law allows, include words of your own that send the strongest signal possible, such as "Patrolled, Prosecuted". If legal, include the law's maximum trespassing fine. In our area, the maximum fine for trespassing is $250. This is spelled out in black and yellow on every sign we post. Even though judges often slap trespasser's hands with a warning or token $50 fine, stating the maximum penalty makes trespassers think twice.

Carry one of your signs into court to show the judge what the trespasser ignored. This reminds the judge that the fine doesn't always have to be $50 and helps you get the maximum fine imposed on trespassers. It has worked for us several times.

Yellow signs are the most visible. White signs don't show well in snow. If you have property along public roads, keep your signs visible by mowing roadsides and trimming around sign trees.

This landowner is tough on trespassers. He not only posts his property, but surrounds it with one strand of wire fencing and a 20-foot-wide patrol road. There is no "accidental" trespassing here.

Don't skip open spaces just because you don't have a tree to hammer a sign onto. Fields and open spaces require metal or pressure treated wooden posts. Another option might be utility poles, but check with the company that owns them before fastening posters to them.

The key is to do this job right the first time. Your entire effort must demonstrate a basic fact: If you're serious enough to maintain your boundaries, you're serious enough to prosecute anyone who trespasses.

"Not on My Land, You Don't"

If you don't think posting signs is enough to discourage trespassers, run a strand of wire along your boundary. Better yet, put up a fence. A poster in the trespasser's face and wire behind it is difficult to ignore.

Also signal your presence by laying down fresh tracks on an access road or patrol road. This sends the message that someone is around and nobody better try anything. One of the first things we do on a hunting weekend is lay down fresh tracks in the mud or snow around our boundaries to intimidate would-be trespassers. This might sound extreme, but it helps to be proactive.

Hire a Person to Patrol for You

If you're uncomfortable encountering trespassers, hire someone to do it for you. Go to a law enforcement officer and explain your needs. Ask for recommendations on how to hire a security person. They probably know one or more deputies who would help in exchange for pay, hunting privileges or both. This is especially true if you're managing for quality deer. We hired a sheriff the first

When dealing with trespassers, firmly but politely ask for identification. Write down the pertinent information, as well as a description of the trespasser. Then ask them to leave your property. Avoid confrontation at all costs. Leave that to the law.

three years during gun season, and he had everyone who came near the place looking over his or her shoulders. The sheriff patrolled the woods and spread the word in town. Every outlaw knew to go elsewhere. We still use hired security on our property, because it is impossible to be there every day of the hunting season. It's one more no-nonsense way to show we're serious about stopping trespassers.

Smile You're on Candid Camera

We know of quite a few land owners who have put their deer cams to work photographing trespassers. This really seems to deter the bad guys. The cameras work day and night and can be set up anywhere. Don't use flash cameras to pinch trespassers as they will see the flash and steal the camera. It is also a good idea to hide the cameras if used for surveillance. We recently lost a $1,000 high-end infra-red deer camera to a trespasser. The camera was set up in an open food plot for a deer census. The trespasser accidentally walked in front of it and because it was out in the open he noticed it. Knowing he had been photographed he had "no choice" but to destroy the evidence by walking away with the camera. Next time the good camera will be hidden and the "decoy" in the open will be a noisy old junker.

Prosecuting Trespassers is a Must

No one wants uninvited trespassing, yet many landowners are reluctant to enforce the laws. We encountered trespassers the first year we owned our property, just as Willis had warned us. Although we heavily posted the property, we encountered several trespassers on opening week of gun season. Being an absentee landowner and wanting to appear reasonable, we granted them one warning. We took down their names and license information, and told them this was their one "get-out-of-jail-free card". We told them if we encountered them again we would prosecute. This

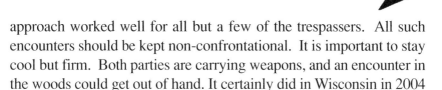

approach worked well for all but a few of the trespassers. All such encounters should be kept non-confrontational. It is important to stay cool but firm. Both parties are carrying weapons, and an encounter in the woods could get out of hand. It certainly did in Wisconsin in 2004 when five hunters were shot and killed by a trespasser.

Here's what we recommend: During the first encounter, explain your program, your expenses, etc., and state that no one enters the property without permission. Then ask the trespasser to leave. Chances are he will ask to finish the hunt. Do not give in, and do not grant permission to stay the rest of the day. If you show any willingness, the game will start. Tell him you and your friends are hunting, and you don't want to create a dangerous situation for anyone, including the trespassers.

Also, do not grant permission to hunt later in the season. Make it clear the next time they're found on the property they will be arrested. We have had a few repeat offenders, as will you, too. During our second year of enforcement, we had two individuals who didn't heed the first warning and came back the next year. The

Fines will solve 99 percent of trespassing problems. We know of countless cases where trespassing is common simply because trespassers don't take the landowner seriously. Without prosecution, trespassing becomes a game.

conversation was short and not too sweet: "Sorry to see you again, Bub. We told you last year we would prosecute you and now you leave us no choice". Again, we took back-tag information and told the hunter to leave. The conservation officer wrote them up later that week and we pressed charges.

In states where back-tags are not required, ask for identification. Write everything down, as well as a description of the trespassers. Many chronic violators hunt with phony IDs and licenses, because they have already lost their hunting license. If the person refuses to divulge anything, remember as many details as possible, including the type of gun or bow he was using. Find his vehicle and get its license number. Authorities can easily trace a license number. Don't be a detective or a hero. Once you get the identification, simply contact a sheriff or conservation officer and report the violation. Let the law work.

If you say you're going to prosecute, you must do so. If you don't, trespassers will call your bluff and not take you seriously, and neither will law-enforcement officers. Sheriffs and game wardens are not social workers and they do not like "counseling" trespassers. They shouldn't have to spend their time issuing warnings. Asking them to have a little talk with a repeat trespasser is usually a waste of their time and yours.

This officer is too busy to be called out to your property just to issue warnings. If the officer recommends an arrest, do your part and follow through with a complaint.

GROW EM RIGHT GUIDE TO FOOD PLOT
827802000348   19.99 T

SUBTOTAL $19.99
SALES TAX 8.25% $1.65
TOTAL $21.64
MASTERCARD $21.64
XXXXXXXXXXXX8271
EXPIRY: XX/XX SWIPED
AUTH# 213250

Receipt required for all
Returns and Exchanges

ITEMS 1
08-28-2008 14:56:26   0402 24-635197 1482

LET US KNOW HOW WE'RE DOING
visit www.gandermountain.com
and click on customer service
or call 1-866-635-2014
we appreciate your feedback!

Shopping at

Gander Mountain will gladly refund or exchange your purchase within 90 days with this receipt as proof of purchase.

*See Store for exceptions.

Thank You for Shopping at

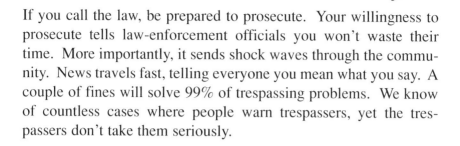

If you call the law, be prepared to prosecute. Your willingness to prosecute tells law-enforcement officials you won't waste their time. More importantly, it sends shock waves through the community. News travels fast, telling everyone you mean what you say. A couple of fines will solve 99% of trespassing problems. We know of countless cases where people warn trespassers, yet the trespassers don't take them seriously.

Without prosecution, it becomes a game. The violator is having fun and your deer management program is a joke. The deer you're trying to grow are shot or chased off your land. Worse, you and your guests are put in danger, not knowing the whereabouts of every hunter on your property.

Denying Permission Requires Tact ... Usually

When encountering a trespasser, it's easy to get angry and lose your cool. Trespassers use up valuable hunting time, steal game and endanger everyone. But you must remain calm and in control. Use firm but convincing language. We point out that they created a dangerous situation for our guests, themselves and us. We tell them we don't tolerate trespassing.

What do you do when politely approached by a solid citizen? Be a good neighbor. This is where tact and good responses are important, especially if the one seeking permission is a neighbor. If you're an absentee landowner, it's even more important to get along with the locals. The answer will usually be "no", but your job is to deliver the "no" in a manner that shows you're an OK guy who just isn't in a position to allow others to hunt your property.

The challenge is to get your neighbors to play by your rules? For those who ask permission, you should politely decline and perhaps offer an explanation. We've had success with this explanation: "We're going to be hunting here with our friends and family. If you're hunting our property, where will we hunt? We don't have

When strangers are good enough to ask permission to hunt, provide them with a courteous, reasonable explanation if you're inclined to say no. You might work with this person in the future as you undertake your management program or hire security personnel. Reasonable people accept, "Sorry, but I can't." They'll still be friends in the future. Jerks are another matter all together.

anywhere else to go". "We're doing a deer management program and have deer sanctuaries that are off limits to everyone. We rest the property on specific days and only shoot certain deer. We can't allow others to hunt. It's all regulated. We have invested a lot of money in this property for hunting."

If the person is still not convinced, we try this one: "If you really have to hunt here, maybe we can work out a business agreement where you share expenses. For 50 percent of our expenses, maybe we can talk. We put thousands of dollars into this place each year, and some financial help might be welcomed." That usually sends them packing.

Some persist and persist and persist. A firm "No, and I do mean no," is about all you can do. As they walk away, remind them the property is patrolled and trespassers will be prosecuted.

Creating Access for Your Use

Enough said on denying access. Let's move onto a more pleasant topic: creating access to your property. Without access, it is virtually impossible to manage a property – especially if you plan to plant food plots and conduct habitat development projects. It's very helpful to have a substantial travel route through your property to do food plots and other work.

You should be able to travel this road with pickup trucks and tractors pulling moderate-sized implements. One of your goals should be to develop a road network that follows your boundaries. A patrol road on a boundary doubles as an access road. Place these roads 10 to 15 yards inside the boundary, so you can check for trespassers. If the road runs directly on the boundary line, neighbors will walk it.

Ready access is important to meeting habitat development goals. It's desirable to lay out a network of roads that create access to all of your project areas. A main road with spurs is effective. You don't want your main access road to cross food plots, browse-cuts or secret hunting spots. Hunting traffic to and from stands might displace your deer at dawn and dark. Deer will figure out this pattern and associate it with hunting. They might even become nocturnal. Try to create access around those areas and leave deer undisturbed. Even then, go easy on using access roads during hunting season.

Create Adequate Access for Farm Equipment

As you plan projects, develop two types of access: hunting access and farming or working access. To do serious farming or food plot work, you need roads to transport equipment and implements. These should be about 15 feet wide to accommodate large implements, and fertilizer and lime trucks. It takes all weekend to lime and fertilize a few acres with small spreader equipment and 50 pound bags of pelleted lime – which is four times as costly as bulk

This bulk-lime truck spreads 12 tons of lime over five food plots in about 30 minutes. The same job took two back-breaking days with smaller equipment and bagged lime. Without good access roads, no lime can be spread with a bulk truck like this.

lime. But it can be accomplished in less than 30 minutes and at a fraction of the cost when done by a commercial application truck.

Keep major access roads away from wet spots, because you will use them heavily during the wet season in spring. If you can't avoid wet areas, drain them or build up your road with rock or gravel. It's also important to note that summer stream crossings can be far different in late fall and early winter. Fordable streams can turn into raging torrents, which shut down a hunt before it starts. Build good bridges or, better yet, avoid water altogether as driving through water creates erosion and can be very tough on equipment.

Create Secondary Roads and Trails for Hunting

In our experience, deer are not too alarmed by motorized traffic on regularly used routes. Establish a traffic pattern through the

This ATV trail winds throughout the entire property. Such trails provide hunters with ready access, and deer become acclimated to the disruption. It's important to stay on the trail and not surprise deer by wandering around on foot.

year to develop a sense of familiarity with the deer using your property. It is important that they have human encounters in the off-season that are not associated with predation. We want deer to see our John Deere Gator and ATV all summer. We want them to encounter us on foot in specified areas only. They just slip out of the way and let us pass, and then go back to their business. We condition them to exhibit the same behavior in the fall when we head out to our hunting locations. They may know we are there but at least they don't head for the neighbors.

If you plan to establish a pattern with deer and vehicles, don't stop, stare and gawk from your vehicles, because this alarms deer. Wave and keep driving. Take hunters to a stand with a familiar vehicle – a pickup truck or four-wheeler – and pick them up the same way.

Stay on Known Roads and Trails

Do everything possible not to surprise deer on your property. Surprise encounters with whitetails send them running, and spooked deer can run a long way. A hunter on foot is much more alarming that a familiar vehicle using a regular route. When we conduct the first tours of the year at the Demo Center, we surprised some deer. Later, we don't see any. They learn to pattern our tour. They hang back or stay bedded until we pass through. Never get off a vehicle and shoot or pursue game, even if it's legal. This can undo your patterning in a hurry. If you don't believe us, spend some time around deer that have been "hunted" from motorized vehicles. Chances are you'll seldom see a deer.

These deer may not act overly alarmed but they do know you are on the property and they will pattern you. This is especially true in hunting season when mature deer are on constant "red alert".

This is when they really use their ears to help keep track of the comings and goings around them. Jerry Martin and Neil both agree that sound really matters in hunting season. Especially strange sounds like metal on metal and briars on nylon. This really sets them off. But, you also need pay attention to familiar sounds like the sounds made while accessing your property with ATVs and trucks. Neil believes that mature deer know when and where you are hunting by where you park your truck or how fast you climb a hill with an ATV. The solution? Vary your routine. Approach your hunting set up from a different direction; park in a different spot. Take the ATV instead of the truck or better yet, walk. Moving deer rely heavily on their noses. Bedded deer are all ears and can figure out what's going on without leaving their beds.

Access is an important management concept. Legitimate access facilitates management and makes hunting easier and more

fun. Illegal access is a major problem and aggressive steps must be taken to eliminate it. Both require planning and action. Give it plenty of thought and do it right the first time.

Chapter V

Logging Roads and Clearings

The tram crawls down an old logging road that has been trans-formed into a smorgasbord of food for white-tailed deer. The road's 12-foot wide center is ankle deep in lush clover and chicory. Stump shoots, brambles, berries, forbs and other browse species grow 15 yards on both sides of the road. An occasional brush pile provides a home to ground critters, while old snag trees, ravished by wood-peckers, are homes to cavity-nesting birds. It was not always this way. Eight years before, this road was canopied, barely passable, and devoid of deer food. It was typical of most woodland roads. It was well on its way to becoming one with the surrounding woods, and years beyond producing usable food or cover.

In wooded areas, property owners often lack open space to plant or create deer forage. However, logging roads and clearings - created by a variety of disturbances - can usually be found in most wooded areas where other open space is scarce. They might be bushy and cluttered with new growth, but they can usually be cleared. These areas are priceless. They not only provide access,

This skidder is making a mess, but this logging road will be converted into a green ribbon of nutritious clover within three months. The main road will be planted, and the roadside will be allowed to grow up in brush, creating a whitetail hotspot.

but they can also be converted to valuable feeding areas, capable of producing tons of nutritious forage.

Developing Logging Roads and Clearings

Many logging roads and woodland clearings have good soil and moisture. Therefore, they can be planted with high-quality perennial seeds. Chickory and clover blends like Chicory Plus™ from the Whitetail Institute make an excellent logging road forage. Planting logging roads is simple, but you must follow basic agricultural practices. That is, the soil must be fertile, moist and have a pH of around 6.0 or above. Acidity is often high in woodlands, especially when oaks with their acidic leaves dominate the area. In most cases, roads near oaks and acid-producing conifers need lime applications. Planted areas also need a minimum of three to four hours of direct sunlight each day to ensure adequate growth, especially in spring and summer. If you have logging roads you want

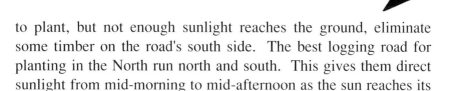

to plant, but not enough sunlight reaches the ground, eliminate some timber on the road's south side. The best logging road for planting in the North run north and south. This gives them direct sunlight from mid-morning to mid-afternoon as the sun reaches its zenith.

Planted logging roads are especially valuable in summers when hot, drought-like conditions prevail. Because logging roads usually are found near shade-producing trees, they get a break from the scorching summer sun. The partial shade provided in summer keeps logging roads on our Demo Center in full production from June through August, long after our sun-baked food plots go dormant from heat and drought.

Planting Equipment

Logging roads can be worked with a variety of cultivating tools, from tractor-drawn disks to ATV equipment. Landowners who

Most ATV equipment works well on logging roads. Be sure to buy high-quality equipment. You don't want broken-down equipment ruining a weekend you set aside for planting food plots.

Heavy-duty logging equipment creates miles of logging roads that can easily be planted. Planting perennial forages will boost your plant production. Remember, every 1200 yards of logging road equals one acre of field.

don't own farm equipment and tractors can do a decent job developing logging roads with a 500c.c. ATV and a heavy duty ATV disc. Unlike a couple of years ago, many high quality ATV implements are available on the market today. Our website (www.north-countrywhitetails.com) features some of the best.

Logging roads allow you to generate forage in remote areas that cannot be reached with farming equipment. One of our NorthCountry clients has had great success developing woodland clearings and logging roads into feeding areas. First, he leveled and worked the logging roads with ATV implements. Two weeks later, he used an herbicide similar to Roundup® to kill the remaining weeds and seedlings. Because of soil conditions and the dense oak woods surrounding the roads, his soils are acidic and require lime.

He didn't have access to tractors or heavy equipment, but he could get into the area with a four-wheel-drive pickup truck. He took two trips to carry 2 tons of lime in the truck's bed, and backed it into a remote stretch of road. His son drove slowly while he scattered the lime with hand tools. In 25 minutes, he shoveled enough lime to last several years. They also applied fertilizer with a hand spreader. Using ATV implements, he roughed up the road and worked in the lime and fertilizer. The ATV's tires produced a firm seedbed by driving back and forth, a job his son relished. After they seeded the beds, he drove over it again to set the seed.

This logging road planting is miles from the nearest public road, and rivals even the best food plots for quality forage. It is easily hunted and was planted in a half day by its owner.

Because of good moisture and adequate sunlight, the stands of clover and chicory thrived. They were in their fourth year when we wrote this book.

As a result, our friend has a quarter-acre of knee high quality forage tucked into the most remote part of his property. It is surrounded by hardwoods and dense hemlock stands, and is set up perfectly for bowhunting. Deer craving a high protein food source are regular visitors. This set up has produced dozens of deer for the freezer. Best of all, it is miles from a public road.

A logging road covered by lush clover and chicory looks like a green ribbon winding through the woods, and it produces more food than you might think. A typical logging road that's 12 feet wide - wider roads are even better - equals a half-acre every 600 yards. When planted correctly, this much needed road will grow up to 5 tons of quality forage each year. Plant another five or 10 half-acre roads, and you will add significant tonnage of top shelf forage.

A whitetail consumes about 1.5 tons of forage per year. Planting log roads will take the pressure off both your woods and food plots. An added bonus is that logging roads usually make better hunting set ups than food plots.

Basic Plantings for Logging Roads

The proper method for planting logging roads is a simple step-by-step process. Basically, the technique is the same as planting food plots. First, determine the site's fertility with a soil test. Use a pH meter, which costs about $25, or take a soil sample to the farm extension service or land grant university for analysis, which costs $10 to $15. Be sure to indicate the forage varieties you intend to plant, and take your soil sample from several places at depths from 2 - 5 inches. Follow the soil analysis recommendations carefully. Liming and fertilizing will almost always be required to make plants grow better in woodland settings.

This logging road would be improved if all trees within 15 yards of both sides were removed. That would allow sunlight to nurture clover that's planted in the road, and encourage brush to grow on both sides.

Next, use Roundup® or a similar herbicide to kill competing weed growth. After the Roundup® has done its job, it's time to cultivate, disk or use hand tools to disturb the soil. Then, prepare a smooth, firm seedbed by rolling the soil with your ATV's tires or a lawn roller. You can drag almost anything behind the ATV to smooth and even the soil. For instance, an old bedspring works great, as does a 6-foot length of chain link fence. Next, broadcast the seed with an ATV seeder or hand crank seeder. Finally, press the seed into the ground with a roller or the ATV's tires to ensure soil contact. Make sure you do not bury the seed by disking or dragging. Seed buried deeper than an inch or so will die. Once nature adds the water, your plants should be up in a week or so.

Advanced Logging Road Development

A green ribbon of woodland forage is a great improvement to any property and a valuable addition to your habitat program, but a little more work will provide even more browse and four seasons of high quality deer food. For the ultimate logging road project, take it one step further to create a woodland smorgasbord. To do this, cut all trees 10 to 15 yards on both sides of the road, except for valuable timber and "hunting" trees. Leave the stumps and tops for cover and regeneration. Trees cut

The doe at the end of this logging road is barely visible. The surrounding cover provides food and concealment. Deer travel these brush-lined logging roads heavily.

close to the ground (coppiced) produce shoots, and the tops provide security cover and allow browse to regenerate within the protective confines of their limbs. The suddenly abundant sunlight, along with adequate doses of lime and fertilizer, create an ideal environment and tons of food. Just imagine: 15 feet of lush clover bordered on both sides by 30 or more yards of dense, high quality browse winding through you wood lot. That's why we call woodland roads smorgasbords. In fall and winter, these places make ideal hunting spots, especially if you leave "hunting trees" along the roadways, and deer have a reason to use them year round.

Our Demo Center has almost 50 miles of logging roads, many of which have been seeded and developed. However, not all logging roads are suitable for high quality seeds. When we develop a lengthy stretch of road, we apply the highest grade seeds in the most choice, moist areas with the best soil. Clover and chicory are ideal plantings when you find good growing conditions on logging roads.

Woodland openings create brush. Brush creates browse. Browse creates deer. This deer is eating the tips off twigs, where 90 percent of the twig's usable nutrition is found. Note the already-browsed twig above his left eye.

In dry, thin soils, we apply erosion mixes that consist of less expensive seeds. These sites will green up, but they might not turn into high quality forage. Generic brands of clover, rye grass and birdsfoot trefoil provide a good mix of forage in marginal conditions. Planting logging roads yields two bonuses: deer use them to some degree, and the vegetation prevents erosion and road wash out.

The new brush growth along your road edges also produces a privacy screen for deer, making them feel secure as you travel the road. If you often use the roads during the off season and condition deer to your presence, you can sneak into your stands during the hunting season without alarming nearby deer.

Log roads can be difficult to establish so it is extra important to keep them producing year after year. Clover and chicory-based roads should be mowed when weeds flower and before they go to seed.

Invading grasses should be treated with a grass killing herbicide like Poast™ or Arrest™. Arrest comes in small quantities, which makes it handy for food plotters. Clover only roads can be treated with Slay™ (be sure to use a surfactant) to kill broad leaf weeds but do not use it on chicory. Slay and Arrest should not be mixed and applied at the same time. Spray one chemical, refill the tank and spray the next.

ATV sprayers will spray approximately 12-15 gallons of water per acre at a speed of 4mph. Keep your speed constant at 4mph load your sprayer with 25-30 gallons of solution and you are all set to spray 2,400 yds. (2 acres) of road.

Log Landings and Woodland Clearings

Every logging operation creates and uses some type of a cleared work area. Loggers call these sites landings or log decks. We call them miniature food plots. Like abandoned logging roads, they are

This small food plot was created on a log landing. These deer are secure in this out-of-the-way "mini-plot." In fact, whitetails seem to prefer such sites over large fields.

usually covered with brush and young trees. But if they are less than 10 years old or even a bit older, they can be cleared in a day or so with hand tools, or in an hour or two with a bulldozer.

These mini-plots are usually acidic because of sawdust and log bark left behind from the logging operation, but they can be converted into food producing areas. Typically, log decks have shallow, compacted, infertile soil because of intensive work, but this can be fixed. Liming and fertilizing helps, as does roughing up the compacted soil. The right amount of lime allows more growth, and seeding with clovers when the ground is thawing in spring - known as "frost seeding" - helps knit bare spots together. In most cases, it's undesirable to plow and disk too much, because these areas have often lost most of their topsoil from the heavy equipment traffic, and what remains is usually too compacted for optimum growing conditions.

Rather than repeatedly disturb marginal erosion prone soils, it's often better to frost seed a mixture of hard seed on the snow or

This buck is working the edge of a small woodland clearing. Bucks like him prefer to stay back from large open spaces. He didn't grow to this size by spending many daylight hours in the open.

Photo by Charles J. Alsheimer

frozen ground in early spring, and then control the weeds with selective herbicides. Note, when frost seeding; expect germination rates of at least 30 per cent of the seed, but not as much as with normal cultivation. The goal is to grow something green for deer, and to reach the point where natural seeding takes over. This allows you to get a food source established while gradually improving the soil's growing potential through mowing, or even by spreading topsoil or manure.

Once you get the green stuff growing, don't redo it too often. Because log landings often have fragile soil, mow the area to add organic matter to improve soil quality. It might not perform like a high quality food plot, but it will produce valuable forage for whitetails and can be improved over time. Manure adds to the soil production, as do leaves, hay bales or any other organic matter you find. Shred it with a rotary mower for rapid decomposition. Eventually, after you have rebuilt the soil's organic layer, you can establish high quality perennials like Imperial Whitetail Clover.

Work with What You Have

Let's face it: Not every recreational property has several fields that can be used exclusively to grow high quality deer forage. If your property has few open spaces, do what you can to create more openings and work with what you have. If you have the fortunate choice of developing a food plot or a logging road, put your money into the food plot. If you are not blessed with open, tillable soils and areas that can be developed into food plots, work with what you have, wherever you find it.

Not everybody is blessed with open, tillable soils and areas that can be easily developed into food plots. Work with what you have wherever you find it. You will be amazed at the success you can acheive.

You will be amazed by the success you can achieve. The miles of logging roads on our Demo Center equal many acres of food plots. We haven't planted it all, because we prefer to develop tillable food plots in open space. Even so, we have planted more than half our roads in some type of green forage.

Best of all, the deer don't seem to know the difference, especially those huge, secretive bucks that survive by staying out of harm's way.

Chapter VI

Creating Sanctuaries

The NorthCountry tram is creeping through the center of the property. You begin seeing yellow signs to your left. The diamond shaped signs are spaced more closely than you expect. Why are they here in the center of a property? The signs separate dense, impenetrable brush from more open terrain. The access road runs between. We can only guess what lies behind the sign, because humans have crossed the boundary marked by these signs only twice in the past 15 years. We know by trails and tracks that deer use this place heavily, especially during gun season, and sometimes we see them in the brush as we pass. We also see signs of huge bucks nearby. You're looking at one of several sanctuaries at the NorthCountry Demo Center. No one goes beyond these signs, but that was not always the case. Before the early 1990s, the sites were hunted heavily. Hunters put on deer drives through the area, and by the middle of gun season, deer could not be found in these parts.

If you want mature whitetails on your property, you must keep some areas off limits to humans. Actually, we create two kinds of sanctuaries: working sanctuaries and absolute off limits sanctuaries. To appreciate the latter, let's follow a doe and her button buck fawn.

Soon after buying our land, we laid out a 15-acre sanctuary. A year or two later, a doe finds this thick bedding area that humans avoid. She knows danger lurks on the property, but she feels safe there. So does her fawn. In fact, her fawn has never encountered a human in this secure area.

A year later in spring, her buck fawn leaves the property at the doe's urging, feeling the need to disperse. He leaves home and takes up residence two miles away. But, he remembers where safety lies, and eventually returns to the sanctuary when people pressure increases during hunting season. The doe goes back to the sanctuary as well. The next season, as a 2 ½ -year old buck, he is again elsewhere, living and searching for does, but the opening of

This doe will raise many fawns in this sanctuary during her life. Many of them will be bucks that might return to the site as mature deer when hunting pressure rises. One or two dispersing bucks might even stumble onto the sanctuary and take up permanent residence.

102

gun season brings a major influx of noise and human activity. The 2 ½ -year old buck remembers the haven and returns. He moves in and out of it, to and from food plots, but almost always at night.

Fast forward four years. Our fawn is a trophy buck, and the urge to disperse has left him. He has become the dominant buck in the area, seldom straying far or long from this sanctuary. He might be nocturnal, but you know he's there because he leaves tracks and rubs as he comes and goes. Sooner or later, a doe will tempt him during her magical 48-hour period. He will lose all caution and run her into one of our hunting areas.

Sanctuaries should be clearly designated. This keeps guests from inadvertently entering the restricted area. Placing safe havens for away from property boundaries helps keep trespassers out. We use these specially-designed aluminum signs.

As long as you don't violate the sanctuary, a big buck will continue to use it. Outside of the sanctuary, you might encounter him on any hunt and maybe see him once per season. That's how we define quality deer hunting.

The sanctuary has created a quality hunting situation. We might see this monster only once or twice a season. A four or five year old animal is as good as it gets on this property. We know he is there and we're confident we will eventually see him. As long as we do not violate the sanctuary, the big buck continues to use it. Outside of the sanctuary, we might encounter him once per season, that's how we define quality deer hunting. The sanctuary has helped keep the high-quality buck on our 500 acre property, and given us a better chance of harvesting a trophy animal.

Locating Sanctuaries

Natural sanctuaries are often overlooked by hunters, but they occur everywhere. They can be nearly vertical side hills, wide medians in a highway, weed lots behind the barn, or one acre overgrown building lots. Some four and five year old bucks are out there, and that's where they hide during the season.

The good news is that you don't have to start hunting median strips on highways. You can hold quality deer on your property if you create a safe haven. Off limits sanctuaries require complete protection. Don't risk visits by lost hunters or hikers,paint the trees and hang signs. We created sanctuary signs to alert our hunters that they're about to enter a sanctuary. Our website has signs for sale. For a sanctuary to live up to its name, deer must have thick cover and food. Give the deer what they need, and they will stay.

A working sanctuary is a site where we create habitat during the off season. We enter these areas only during the off season, typically during the winter. Even then, we enter them as little as possible, and only to cut trees to create cover and food. As the fawning season approaches, we avoid these areas completely, leaving them as deer havens. It remains that way through hunting season.

Entering a Sanctuary

If a wounded deer enters a sanctuary, we track it only at night. We go in with a lantern and no more than two individuals. Our entrance is low-key, with no shouting or loud talking, you'll never

Neil shows off two consecutive years of antlers from this buck. The sheds were found within 500 yards of each other. The buck was killed on a clover food plot less than 100 yards from a "working sanctuary." The sanctuary was home to this big fella for at least three years, and probably more, because he was 5-1/2 when shot.

hear us yell, "Hey Joe, over here". By tracking only at night, we give deer a chance to sneak out under the cover of darkness. Chances are, in fact, they left the sanctuary as darkness descended, and won't be spooked at all. Deer can still return during darkness without risk of being killed by neighbors, and if you're lucky, they won't cut your tracks or know you violated their home. Avoid any daylight impact during autumn. Do not, under any circumstances, risk chasing deer from a sanctuary during daylight. It might be the end of the 5 ½-year-old buck you worked so hard to keep at home.

Laying Out Sanctuaries

Sanctuaries do not have to be large. A 5-acre sanctuary is sufficient to hold a mature white-tailed buck. The thicker the sanctuary, the more animals it can hold. Its size also determines how many mature animals hole up there. For hunting, it's best to lay out

Locating food plots close to sanctuaries increases the odds of catching a hungry buck outside of the site. It also concentrates does, which will lure him out during the rut.

several small sanctuaries rather than one big centralized haven, allowing you to hunt travel corridors between the havens.

Try not to put sanctuaries near property boundaries because they're easily violated. People might wander in by mistake, take a shortcut, or walk past your signs in the dark. Sanctuaries lose their effectiveness even if violated once a year. One or two trips through the sanctuary can eliminate 10 years of off-limits discipline on your part. Mark the boundary and mark it well. Make sure recreational and hunting guests know this rule is inflexible. Zero tolerance!

Have our sanctuaries worked? Year after year, we see signs of huge bucks near these sites. We never know when a buck will walk out. Craig saw one such buck just once two years ago. He had just arrowed a nice 120 class 2 ½-year old buck when out of nowhere a monster buck appeared. Craig watched through binoculars as this incredible animal, half again as large as the 2 ½-year-old buck (who

Having entered a sanctuary, this buck will relax for the day. While in the sanctuary, he is in no danger from hunters. Although it is tempting to go in after him, it would be a huge mistake to do so.

was now bedded) took a run at the wounded buck. Talk about domination. The mortally wounded deer jumped up, ran 40 yards and crashed into a brush pile. The monster stared at the "little guy" and slowly drifted off toward some does feeding on acorns. Every year we spot a couple of sanctuary bucks. They come and go like ghosts. Mostly we see their tracks and rubs.

Sanctuaries are easy habitat-development projects to implement. Once you locate it and mark it off-limits, you need do little more than avoid it. We also try to create and maintain a food plot or two near or between two sanctuaries to entice a trophy buck to leave the haven for a bite, or more likely to check out does that work the plots almost constantly.

You can hunt the edges of the sanctuary with tree stands, or have a travel road around it. Deer learn they are safe and use it regularly as long as they are never surprised there or sense humans nearby are trying to kill them.

Sanctuary Size

How big should sanctuaries be? Well, a neighboring property of 300 acres has a 20-acre sanctuary laid out in a way that allows easy observation from a distance. Every year the owner, Randy, watches deer running to his sanctuary from high-pressure neighboring properties when the guns start going off. Randy said the deer get 30 to 40 yards inside, and then immediately relax, browse, bed down and hang around 100 yards inside. They stay until early evening, and then head back out to feed. He is able to watch deer in his sanctuary and is certain they just unwind once inside its boundaries. We sometimes wonder if Randy spends more time observing deer in his sanctuary than hunting, but that is what quality deer hunting is all about.

Sanctuaries are easy habitat projects to design and complete. Basically, once you locate it and mark it off-limits, you need do little more than avoid it.

Woods sanctuaries should be larger than brush sanctuaries because a sanctuary really doesn't start until a deer can no longer see you from inside the sanctuary. This is often called his security zone. An un-harassed deer is typically not secure in the open woods until he is about 75 yards from where a person might pass by. Conversely, in heavy brush a deer can be secure 15 yards from where a person might pass.

Our 500-acre property has three 15-acre off-limits sanctuaries. One is our original sanctuary, and the second became a sanctuary by default because there's no effective way to hunt it. We declared it off-limits about six years after buying the land. When laying out a sanctuary, select places where the wind swirls, or where topography creates a difficult hunting situation. Such places make good sanctuaries, especially if they're dominated by dense, heavy cover. If you spook more deer than you see in a tough hunting area, why not let deer have that area and restrict deer/human encounters to the outskirts? In addition to our two main sanctuaries, we also have several 1-to 2-acre havens we never enter and of course, a half-dozen or so working sanctuaries. In total, we probably have up to half of our property in some form of "off-limits" program.

Neil likes to set up sanctuaries so as to tempt mature bucks to travel from safe haven to safe haven. This increases the chances of getting one of these beauties in your sights during daylight hours. The more property layout work Neil does the more sanctuaries he seems to use. He frequently recommends that up to 30% of a property be turned into sanctuary. We also believe that the smaller the property the higher percentage of the property should be sanctuary. This is hard for some landowners to swallow but in high-pressure areas it's the only way to go. A rule of thumb: the older age class of deer you want to hold on your property, the higher percentage of the total property should be in sanctuary. Want to hold 5 ½-year old bucks? Dedicate 50% to 75% of your property to sanctuaries. 2 ½-year old bucks, 20%-30%. Sounds extreme but it isn't; not if you want to keep big bucks on your property.

We are especially cautious around our sanctuaries during gun season. We try not to encounter deer that are coming to and going from our sanctuaries during this time of vulnerability. We cut the bucks a lot of slack during the second half of gun season because, in our view, they've just about made it another year. Sometimes by the end of the season, we're actually rooting for a particular buck to make it through, so we might thrill at his tracks and rubs when the next season approaches.

A big part of quality deer hunting is the thrill of anticipation. Sanctuaries are all about keeping mature deer on your property and waiting for them to suddenly appear. A couple of years ago, Craig took 154" five year old who appeared out of no where on a clover plot fifteen minutes before the end of gun season one snowy evening. He spent the last 3 years of his life in a nearby sanctuary. We have the sheds to prove it. That's what makes hunting fun, and what gets you out of bed every morning. That's quality deer hunting, and what sanctuaries can do for your deer program.

Chapter VII

Woods Working - TSI

It's September, and the NorthCountry tram just entered a beautiful stand of hardwoods. The first of millions of acorns are beginning to fall in a 25-acre woodlot of red and white oaks. Virtually every oak in the woods is loaded with the whitetail's favorite mast crop. Looking up to assess the acorns, you see ample daylight penetrating the oaks' canopy. An occasional stump suggests a chainsaw has been working here. The woodlot and its wildlife are the better for it. Brushy cover obscures the ground.

This is a prime example of "timber stand improvement," or TSI for short. But seven years before, this was not the case. The oak canopy was overcrowded and intertwined. Acorn production was marginal; the oak's growth had slowed and virtually no food or cover could be found on the forest floor because sunlight was blocked out. With more than 50 percent of our property in hardwoods, we were losing money and our wildlife was suffering. We had to start working to improve our woodland habitat.

Deer get a great deal of their food from browsing even when lush crops grow near browse sources. Woodlands are important to whitetails and often dominate deer hunting properties. Improving your woodlands through TSI is a critical part of any management plan and should be practiced by most landowners.

Deer get a great deal of their food from browsing even when lush crops grow near browse sources. Woodlands are important to whitetails and can dominate properties.

Timber Stand Improvement: Haircut for the Woods

In its simplest form, TSI is nothing more than a thinning haircut for your woodlot. Double and triple trunk trees usually are reduced to singles and undesirable trees cut to make room for qual-

Photo by Charles J. Alsheimer

Acorns are a preferred source of whitetail food. Deer heavily consume them in autumn. Timber stand improvement projects increase acorn production, and allow sunlight to reach the forest floor to stimulate new growth.

ity trees. Foresters continually look up while marking trees for TSI. They want to thin the canopy enough so remaining trees have ample room to grow. They want to see blue sky surrounding the still standing treetops when the thinning is finished. Selective thinning increases sunlight; creating a healthier stand of trees by accelerating the growth of existing timber, and permitting ground cover to regenerate.

Oaks produce more acorns if they're thinned. In an uncrowded woodlot, valuable understory will be lush providing browse and cover. TSI inspires a growth spurt for remaining trees, moving them closer to becoming mature saw-log timber; which can be turned into cash for additional habitat projects or land purchases.

People Habitat is Not Deer Habitat

Many of our Demo Center visitors "ooh and ahh" at a few thinned red-pine stands we left untouched on our tour route. They look at neat rows of bare trunks and the carpet of brown needles and say, "Isn't that a nice area!" Well, it might be nice for a stroll or a summer picnic, but it's relatively useless as whitetail habitat. Our friends, the Buckley's, call this "People Habitat". Don't confuse people habitat with deer habitat. The two habitats couldn't be much more different.

TSI is a time-honored, well-established forestry practice. With TSI, everybody wins, landowners and wildlife alike. Although TSI is a simple concept, it is best

Symmetrical rows of tall red pines and a carpet of needles are great for summer picnics, but they do little for deer. This stand should be cut heavily. Exposing the ground to sunlight will produce prime cover in three to five years.

practiced with the assistance and guidance of a professional forester. A professional can mark your woodlot for thinning, and leave the rest up to you, or he can arrange for a crew to come in, and thin the marked stand for you. The forester will know which trees to keep, and which to remove for the woodlot's long term benefit.

When you thin trees, you can expect several positive outcomes. First, it allows remaining trees to accelerate their growth and add valuable board footage. A good working woodlot increases its value seven percent per year, which isn't bad by most investment standards. Hardwoods like oak, cherry, maple and ash, to name a few, can generate major income. Softwood like pine and spruce are also valuable. Besides increasing valuable board footage, TSI creates a healthier collection of trees in the woodlot. Trees left after thinning have adequate room for growth. Their canopies receive unrestricted sunlight, and their roots absorb more nutrients and moisture from the soil instead of sharing them with competing trees. Consequently, these trees are more disease-resistant and produce more mast.

This logger is cutting the poorer of two trees growing from the same bowl. The remaining, higher-quality oak will then grow faster, produce more mast, and become a more valuable saw log at harvest time. Daylight reaching the ground also creates valuable understory.

Thinning woodlots allows valuable sunlight to reach the forest floor. This sunlight creates and stimulates the growth of under-brush, which provides food and cover for many species of wildlife, including deer. As a bonus, if you leave thinned treetops in the woods, they will be browsed the first year by deer, especially if the cutting is done in winter. The tops also provide shelter and cover for other animals, and protect new growth from over-browsing by deer. As we said, everybody wins.

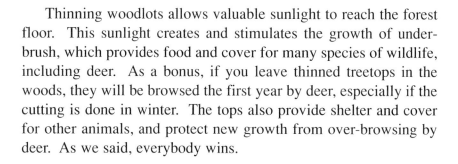

Thinning woodlots allows valuable sunlight to reach the forest floor. This sunlight creates and stimulates the growth of underbrush, which provides food and cover for many species of wildlife, including deer.

Chainsaw Safety

A note on woods work: A chainsaw might be a deer's best friend, yet this tool can be very dangerous to man, especially week-end warriors new to chainsaws and strenuous work. In terms of chainsaw safety, it's wise to assume it's not a matter of, if you will have an accident, but when. Anyone who runs a saw long enough will have some type of mishap. Take steps to protect yourself. The must-have pieces of safety gear include protective chaps and a hard-hat with an eye shield or goggles, and steel-toed boots.

Hearing protection is also mandatory and will reduce fatigue. We deer managers often try to run a saw longer than we should, especially when we only get into the woods a day or two at a time. Fatigue sets in and we force the cutting and end up off balance. The saw can easily find its way to your thigh when your arms are weary. One wrong move and the chain can touch your leg, causing at the least a trip to the emergency room.

Protective chaps will jam and stall the saw before it reaches your skin. Chaps have saved many loggers' legs. The helmet should have an eye shield, and it should be used at all times. Wood chips fly everywhere when running a saw. Saws can also kick back and strike your chest or head.

That all sounds scary, but a larger danger looms overhead. Rotten or hung-up limbs often fall when you start to cut a tree. Loggers call these limbs "widow-makers" for good reason. Even a small limb can deliver a painful, crippling or fatal blow. You will never see it coming, so study what's overhead before starting a cut.

Besides a good chainsaw, you need the right protective gear. This professional cutter has eye, ear and head protection, plus cutting chaps, which will jam a saw before it gets to your leg. His cutting position is well balanced, with the saw away from his body.

It's important to establish chainsaw rules and guidelines for yourself and friends. One good rule is never cut alone. Always work in tandem. It's also smart to take breaks every 15 minutes. Run the saw for short periods and then rest. Don't force the work when you're tired and don't cut with a dull saw. Dull chains tire you quickly and force you to cut off balance by leaning into the cut. It's also hard on the saw.

If you plan to do some cutting, attend a course to learn the proper techniques. Professional loggers from "The Game of Logging" run excellent courses in our area, it might save your life. Neil has cut into his chaps at least twice, each time the saw bound up in the chaps' protective fibers before reaching his trousers.

We have also been clobbered by dead limbs more than once. When we conduct Demo Center tours, we point out where trees will drop and the consequences. Before cutting, study each tree to evaluate its danger. You must also study surrounding trees. Are dead limbs above you? Will they free-fall? Will the supporting branches move? Which direction will the tree fall? Watch leaners and hung-up trees. Depending on how they are stuck, they might be under enormous pressure, and virtually blow apart when cut. They could also bind your chainsaw's bar and force you to use another saw, or a wedge and ax, to get free.

Always cut with another person nearby. Not only is emergency help then at hand, but another person can keep you out of harm's way when saws bind or trees hang up. A partner also helps limit fatigue.

Don't Forget the Fertilizer

Once the chainsaw work has been completed, some believe you gain great benefits by fertilizing trees. We use tree tablets designed to increase mast production. They're easier to use than loose fertilizer, and they supposedly increase acorn yield. Some believe fertilized acorns are more attractive to deer than run-of-the-mill acorns. We're not sure about all the claims, but we enjoy believing it helps. We do know that the oaks bordering our well-fertilized food plots produce better than our deep woods oaks, but that could be due to more than fertilizer.

Apple Trees Need Attention, Too

While we're on the subject of nurturing mast producers, a word about apple trees: The Demo Center has more than 40 "wild" apple trees scattered through its brush lots. When we bought the place in 1990, the seller said there was "one or two" of them. Each year we

These "wild" apple trees were rescued from a slow death 10 years before this photo was taken. We removed surrounding trees and brush, and pruned dead or stressed wood. These trees also get a dose of fertilizer each year.

Photo by Charles J. Alsheimer

This buck in enjoying the fruits of our labor. A little attention to apple trees every year or so helps produce good-looking fruit like this.

do some apple-tree work; most of them were "released" the first 10 years we owned the place. We removed the overstory and cut back competing brush. Each year, we also prune dead limbs and thin the interval limbs to make room for sunlight and encourage air movement, 30% of the branches can be safely removed each year.

We also fertilize our apple trees each spring by making pry-bar holes in the ground near the tree's drip line, and fill them with 5-10-15 fertilizer. We use a half-pound of fertilizer for every 4 inches of tree trunk.

Most of our wild apple trees produce small apples each fall just in time for bow season. Deer pause to sample a few as they come and go between food plots and resting areas.

We don't recommend planting an apple orchard to feed deer, because food plots are much more efficient. But if you're fortunate enough to have "wild" apple trees on your property, do what you can to keep them healthy and producing fruit.

Don't underestimate the importance of wooded areas to deer, and don't underestimate how much quality habitat you can create in the woods. Most of our clients don't do enough work on their wooded areas, even though woodlands are every bit as important to creating quality wildlife habitat as fields and food plots. Best of all, you don't need a lot of fancy tractors and farm implements to achieve your goals. A $500 investment in cutting gear will get the habitat-improvement ball rolling. For that price, you should be able to buy an ax, a few wedges and a semi-professional chainsaw. Don't skimp on safety, you'll also need safety chaps, eye and ear protection, and a helmet to protect you from potentially terrible accidents.

Photo by Charles J. Alsheimer

Chapter VIII

Logging On

You're riding the NorthCountry tram down a woodland road through a mixed oak, hickory and maple forest. Every 40 yards is an 18-to22-inch stump. About 30 feet from each stump lies a severed treetop heavily browsed by deer. In the protection of these treetops, dozens of oak seedlings stretch for daylight. This scene is duplicated throughout this 100-acre stand of hardwoods, and is the result of a select-cut logging operation five years before. Oak regeneration is everywhere. Acorns cover the ground. Other than an occasional treetop and stump, one would not know loggers had been here; they did their job well. But this was not always the case. Twelve years before, loggers made a mess and virtually destroyed another wooded area on the demo site. We learned our logging lessons the first time.

Make no mistake: Logging does not have to be a four-letter word. Timber harvests have a significant place in habitat management, and should be viewed as a vital tool that provides cash while improving habitat. Unfortunately, logging has developed a questionable-to-bad reputation in recent years. Some logging practices have left the woods scarred with irreparable damage. Some loggers have been unscrupulous and taken advantage of landowners. In cases like these, the bad rap is well deserved. However, with the right approach, logging can be a positive management tool.

This landowner is smiling now, but he won't be so happy when he realizes how difficult, if not impossible, it is to repair this heavy-equipment rut. This kind of damage can and must be prevented.

Money from timber sales can be used to purchase equipment like tractors and field implements. We once paid for an entire property purchase with one selective timber harvest. Timber harvests can also provide that much desired road network on your property for free. When you realize you would pay $75 to $125 per hour to rent a bulldozer, it's easy to see how you can get thousands of dollars of access roads as a by-product of a large logging operation.

Finally, logging can improve habitat dramatically. It thins overcrowded timber and drops treetops, allowing daylight to break through to the ground for the first time in years. Wildlife habitat springs up everywhere as cover and food abound. Best of all, you're getting paid for the job, not paying to have it done.

To maximize logging's benefits, you must put on your thinking cap before beginning. Consult your overall management plan to review your goals and objectives. Once you understand how logging fits into your program and you're relatively certain you want to proceed, hire a consulting forester. Share your plan with him so he can help you make critical decisions. A qualified forester ensures you get a good price for your logs. Because most foresters work on a percentage basis, they strive to ensure you get top dollar for your timber by putting the job out to competitive bids. Also,

they make sure logging roads are laid out correctly, and left in a serviceable condition after the job is complete. They are your agent in the woods, your eyes and ears.

After you and your forester agree on your goals, he marks the trees to be cut and bids out the job. Once the bids are in, he reviews them and presents a recommendation. He also steers you clear of fly-by-night loggers. The conventional wisdom is that consulting foresters more than pay for themselves, even with their commissions netted out. Their expertise is important and necessary. You will only harvest a given stand of timber on your property once or twice in your lifetime; best to do it right. When shopping for a forester, check references and ask around for recommendations. This person is critical to your operation.

Make sure your forester understands your management goals. Most foresters are in the business of growing and harvesting tim-

Logging usually improves deer habitat dramatically. It creates food, cover and open spaces. This buck, and others like him, will use this cut-over area for at least eight to ten years.

The services of a consulting forester are a huge asset in a logging operation. They help you get top dollar for your timber and ensure the work gets done correctly.

ber, and some are not sympathetic to the needs of wildlife. We like to leave dead snag trees as nesting sites for birds and critters. Foresters usually remove snags because they can harbor diseases, but we think their value to wildlife usually outweighs those concerns. The occasional aggressive browse-cut is also attractive to wildlife, yet many foresters will not cut that heavily. Understandably, they have been trained to look after the long term productivity and health of the forest and over harvesting can interfere with these goals. A few extra trees removed from a one-acre parcel can create a high quality browse-cut that pays huge benefits to your wildlife program. We often do clear-cuts to create better cover and food. Clear-cuts also tend to concentrate deer and influence their travel patterns. When it comes to your woods, you're the boss. Remember that!

The highest bidder is not always the best choice when selecting a cutter. Some times they bid high because they cut fast and carelessly. Get references and inspect other jobs they have completed. Did they excessively damage existing trees while harvesting others? Did they drop large trees on smaller ones? Did they damage large numbers of trees by "barking" them when "skidding" logs out of the woods? Trees with serious bark damage eventually rot because organisms attack the tree through the damaged area. Did they leave leaning "widow-makers" or "sprung trees" locked and loaded to do bodily harm? Any sign of empty oil cans, filters or other litter (we really hate trash in the woods)?

Logging equipment can create impassable trenches and mud holes but it doesn't have to. Did they do a thorough job cleaning up? Most of these problems can be avoided if loggers show skill and care in the woods. They should leave it in better condition than they found it. You do not have to accept excessive damage from

The highest bidder is not always the best choice when selecting a cutter. Get references and inspect other jobs they have completed.

logging. Sure, some damage occurs, but it can be minimized and your woods should look good when they leave, kind of like a fresh haircut.

We have become so fussy that we request certain cutters for our property. We specify that one cutter, Roger Gee from the Two Rivers Timber Co. of Lindley, New York, do all our cutting. It's not that their other cutters are poor; we're just more comfortable with him because he is the best we've ever seen. He understands our management program and takes the time to do the kind of work that makes us smile. He is also highly productive, moving right along at a money making pace. Don't accept "productivity" excuses for sloppy work, and don't accept a discounted price for your timber just because you want it done right. "Careful" and "productive" are not mutually exclusive terms. Frantic, helter-skelter activity has no place in the logging woods.

Timber management must be done carefully. It will take more than your lifetime for your woodlots to recover from a cutting. A sloppy logging job is like putting your life savings into the hands of a shoddy investor. Timber is part of your financial future. Spend extra time, do your research, and do the job right.

Neil followed four or five cutters and log skidders around one summer running the clean-up bulldozer. Not all cutters are equally skilled and some are bad news. Roger Gee is an artist with a chainsaw, and fells trees exactly where they must go. He removes small trees in the path of those he is felling so the small ones are not left splintered and bent over. Because of his expertise, we have few damaged trees in our woods, tops on the ground are all you see. Our woodlots are beautiful six months after the job is complete.

In contrast, about three years before we bought our land, the former owner logged our property. The loggers worked through 60 days of almost continuous bad weather and severely damaged the woods with heavy equipment. We were not in a position at the time to shut down the logging (or at least we thought so), but we learned one valuable lesson. Not all loggers are created equal.

Skidders and skidder operators are also a critical part of this equation. These huge machines can wreak havoc with your woods

Skidders are huge machines, capable of damaging trees and roads. The man operating this skidder is skilled and careful not to damage our woodlands excessively.

by barking trees and creating mud holes. But short of logging with horses - an entirely acceptable practice, but difficult to find - skidders are a necessary part of the work. Like cutters, not all skidder operators are created equal. The best we have seen is Jim Bridge. Jim and his machine might be big, but he maneuvers it in our woods as if it's a Volkswagen Rabbit. He is mindful of our property, as is his cutting partner, Mike.

A logging contract should address the construction of logging roads, erosion-prevention measures on roads and hillsides, and how the woods should be left when the job is complete.

Your forester will draw up a contract addressing issues such as the construction of logging roads, erosion-prevention measures on roads and hillsides, and how the woods should be left when the job is complete. The contract should include the maximum height that tops and debris can be left on the ground, and specify that damaged trees should be removed and paid for. Splintered or broken trees and hangers, or "widow-makers", must be cut and dropped.

Often overlooked is a performance bond. A certain percentage - about 10 percent of the overall value of the timber - should be held by you to assure the loggers comply with the contract. That way, if they fail to clean up properly, or unreasonably damage your property, you're holding enough money to hire the work needed to put things right in the woods. Loggers hate this practice, but stick to your guns - especially if you don't know your loggers or haven't checked references. Even the best jobs require clean-up work. Unless the job was done on snow covered frozen ground, it usually requires several thousand dollars of bulldozer time to clean up the woods after a job. Holding their money is your insurance the work gets finished.

Logging roads are part of every job. After the job, they should be cleaned up, graded and have erosion-control measures installed. Planting deer forages not only provides food, but helps control erosion. This is where some loggers duck out. Set up a performance bond in escrow to ensure they stick around for the cleanup.

Done correctly, logging can be a great asset to you as a wildlife manager. It yields much needed cash, it enables you to be a good steward of the land and it helps wildlife. Proceed with caution but proceed none the less.

Photo by Charles J. alsheiner

Chapter IX

Food Plots for Feeding

The NorthCountry tram brings you through a narrow access road surrounded by poplar and white birch, but then you break into a clearing where the ground is lush and green. Like a giant football field, the food plot seems to go on forever. It could be hay but a closer look indicates the field contains assorted rich stands of high-quality deer forages, brassicas to the right, clover and chicory to the left, another mixture in the middle. No trees or irregular plantings interrupt the broad expanse. This field has been laid out to produce forage by the ton, and it feeds scores of white-tailed deer. You're looking at one of the feeding plots at the NorthCountry Demo Center. Six years before, this area was five acres of scrub brush. Hawthorne, gray dogwood and scrub pine were abundant. Deer bedded here and eked out a living on browse. That was before we launched our mission to provide high-quality food-plot forages for the deer.

Feeding food plots are designed and managed for agriculture, not hunting. The objective is to produce as much high-quality forage for deer as space permits. We lay out feeding plots for planting efficiency, which minimizes labor and maximizes our return per

This 5-acre feeding plot produces about 50 tons of 30-plus percent protein forage in one year. This keeps the 20-plus deer using it daily in good groceries year-round. Yes, even in winter.

square foot worked. These fields usually cover three or more acres. Our agricultural practices are as close to being commercial as possible, including large equipment and commercial fertilizer and lime applications. We do this to save time and money, and yes, to feed deer. Every night, these "destination feeding plots" are loaded with fat whitetails chomping down 30-plus percent protein forages. They feed deer spring, summer, fall, and well into the winter. Deer from our property, as well as the neighbors' properties, aggressively seek out these forages for their evening meal, and spend most of the night on or near them. That's why we call them "destination plots".

Serious habitat managers usually want to increase the quality and quantity of deer forage on their property; this is the science of food plots. A one-acre high-quality food plot produces tons of 30-plus percent useable protein.

Plots of three or so acres can produce serious tonnage. Some plots are capable of producing 8-10 tons of forage per season. Usable- i.e., digestible - protein is the key, because not all forages have the same digestibility to deer. For instance, medium red

Destination
Feeding Food Plots

N

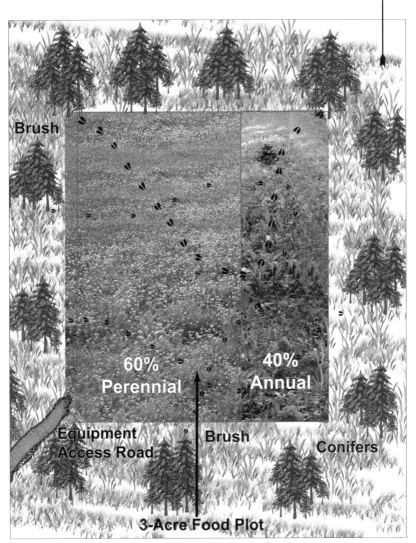

Brush

60%
Perennial

40%
Annual

Equipment
Access Road

Brush

Conifers

3-Acre Food Plot

This feeding food plot is laid out for efficient use of agricultural equipment. It covers three or more acres, and produces tons of highly nutritious forage. It will be planted with perennials and annuals for maximum productivity. Such sites are a favorite destination for whitetails on our property.

clover which is often used in cattle hay mixtures has a high stem content, is much less digestible for deer than most fine-stemmed clovers designed for whitetails.

Feeding food plots should be laid out to accommodate agricultural practices. Plots larger than two acres usually require farm implements, they are too large for ATV equipment. Food plots should be located in areas accessible to farm equipment. For years at the Demo Center we hand-spread fertilizer and lime on inaccessible food plots. We finally got smart and developed a network of heavy-duty roads allowing us to bring in tractors and commercial lime and fertilizer spreaders. By the time we had the road developed, some of the plots had expanded into 5-acre parcels. A lime truck can spread 10 tons of lime in about 30 minutes. This lime costs just over $30 per ton. Before using commercial spreaders, we bought lime in pellet form. It came in 50-pound bags we could handle manually. We hauled it in a pickup truck, and transported it by ATV to a small spinner-type spreader. The process took a weekend to do the same work a lime truck accomplishes in a half-hour.

Access roads allow the commercial spreading of lime and fertilizer. Each year, we save thousands of dollars and hundreds of hours of back-breaking labor by hiring commercial spreaders. This spreading truck will cover a 5-acre plot in no time.

Undesirable grasses are ever present in food plots, and can quickly take over a quality plot. We use a grass-specific herbicide like Arrest™ to keep grasses in check. It will not harm our broadleafs like brassicas, chicory and clover.

Even worse was the cost. Pellet lime costs more than $130 per ton, not to mention the intense labor. Spreading 20 tons a year cost a lot of money and was physically ruinous. We ran off all of our friends who claim they took up golf. That's why access roads are needed to work large plots efficiently.

Feeding food plots should be laid out to accommodate long, straight equipment runs and the large turning radii of medium-sized (30 to 75 hp) tractors pulling 10-to16-foot wide implements. This is best accomplished by designing large rectangular-or square-shaped plots. Uneven edges and islands of trees add interest and aesthetics, but they interfere with efficient cultivation.

In order to meet your goal of providing as much high-quality forage for deer as possible, you must use proven agricultural practices such as liming and fertilizing, as well as grass and weed control. We now understand why most professional growers use modern chemical treatments. We resisted chemical weed control for a time, preferring to go "organic", but by the late 1990s, we accepted chemical treatments of our food plots. We researched the chemicals we use, and believe they're the only way to go, given our goals, objectives and available time.

Before planting, we use an herbicide like Roundup® to kill weeds and grasses. If left unchecked, they will compete with, and eventually destroy, a high-quality forage stand. Midway through the growing season, we apply an herbicide like Poast™ or Arrest™ to reduce grasses and keep the food plots producing lush clovers, chicories and other forages that deer covet. Arrest does not harm broadleaf cultivars. It just works on grasses. Unlike Roundup®, which turns an entire plot brown in a week or so, Arrest is a little subtler. You won't see a brown "kill off" instead you will gradually notice fewer and fewer grasses in your plots. Give it three weeks and the grass will be virtually non-existent.

We also use a broadleaf weed killer called Slay™ to keep our clover plots weed free. Slay must be used with care however as it will wipe out chicory and brassicas as they are both broad leafs. Also, Slay has a residual affect and will continue to work for up to three years. If you intend to keep your plot in clover indefinitely, Slay is your weed solution. If you intend to introduce forages other than clover and alfalfa, you had better use mechanical weed control such as mowing before broadleaf weeds go to seed.

Slay™ and Arrest™ are now available in food plot sized quantities (pints and quarts). This is a huge plus, as up until a year ago it was difficult if not impossible to purchase grass and broadleaf specific herbicides in quantities of less than 2.5 gallons at a huge cost. Food plotters hated to lay out that kind of cash for an acre or two and then have to store a five year supply of chemical. NorthCountry Whitetails (www.northcountrywhitetails.com) handles small sizes. Chemical treatments have been a huge plus to our program. When treated correctly, our plots last for years.

Steps to Food-Plot Construction

The steps for creating quality food plots are the same as steps for most agriculture. First, take soil samples by removing 12 pint-size scoops with a shovel or soil sample auger. Follow and "X" patter across the plot, and put all dirt in one pail. Use the topsoil or subsoil on each plot. Stir and mix the soil, and then remove 1 ½ cups and place it in a poly-bag for analysis. You want the average of a good-cross section of the plot. The soil can be analyzed by an ag extension service, university, or private soil testing service. Most ag stores can help you find a ag extension service in your area. Be sure to indicate what you intend to plant - clover, chicory, etc on the bag, and they will be able to recommend the amount of lime and type of fertilizer to apply per acre.

In most Northern areas, soils are pH deficient on the acidic side. Soils of 4.5 are very acidic, and a 6.5 pH is moderately acidic. A pH of 7 is neutral. Neutral is where you want to be in most cases. If your sample test comes back at 5.2, the acidity is binding nutrients in the soil. The nutrients are there, but the plants cannot use them. Applying lime raises the pH, unbinds the nutrients and allows plants to use them more efficiently. When we apply fertilizer on a low-pH food plot, the plants can use only a portion of the fertilizer. A 5.2 pH food plot might waste 40 percent of the fertilizer applied.

Soil tests are invaluable. Without them, you have no map to follow when applying lime and fertilizer. Do not skip this step!

Lime is vital, but it might take three or more years of lime applications to raise highly acidic soil to the neutral range.

Common indicators in the North of acidic soils are moss, blueberries and conifers. Oaks are also associated with acidic soils. If your dollars are limited, buy lime first and then fertilizer when you have the cash.

After determining the soil's pH, apply herbicides and/or cultivate to kill all weeds and grasses. We apply Roundup® or a glyphosate based generic product first. Glyphosates do not work on dormant plants. We wait until our hardwoods are sprouting dime sized leafs before applying glyphosates to our fields. Herbicides work best when applied to vigorously growing plants. We apply 2 oz. of Roundup per gallon of water assuming our sprayer will apply 12 gallons of liquid per acre (24oz.). Plowing and disking weeds without herbicide treatment is not as effective as applying herbicides first. You almost always see weed and grasses pop up regardless of how thoroughly you plow and disk. Killing weeds with her-

Photo by Tim Kent

Using a herbicide such as Roundup® first is more efficient than plowing and disking first to rid food plots of weeds. It is also more friendly to the soil as disturbed soil is prone to erosion.

bicides is more efficient than trying to eliminate them through cultivation and is why most commercial growers use them.

After the herbicide does its job, which takes about a week or so, it's now time to turn the soil with a plow or disk to work dead matter into the soil and break up dirt clods for a smooth seedbed, which helps prepare a seedbed.

Finally, we smooth and pack the surface with a roller or cultipacker before we seed to remove air pockets and soil fluff which interferes with seed germination and root development. Packing the surface also creates a smooth surface for spreading seeds, and allows the soil to hold moisture and heat. A firm seedbed improves seed germination and produces a better stand of forage.

It's now time for the Weather Channel. It's no accident that farmers have watched the weather for eternity. Ideally, a gentle, day-long rain will arrive as soon as you finish seeding as rain and soil moisture are critical to success. The worst scenario is germi-

This neat food plot has just been cultipacked. It is now ready for seed to be spread. No air pockets or dirt clods will inhibit germination and root development.

An old-fashioned "whirly gig" hand-spreader" does the job with little wasted seed. ATV spreaders are quicker, but must be used carefully so as not to apply too much or too little seed.

nation followed by drought. Tiny seedlings need moisture to survive. Germination followed by drought is fatal to any kind of crop. Timing your seeding pays dividends. Of course, you can play the weather only a few days at a time, but it's worth a try. Beyond that, it's all up to Mother Nature. But remember, nothing happens without moisture and of course too much moisture is almost as bad as too little. No wonder farmers are such patient people.

With rain in the future, it's time to broadcast your seed. Today's food-plot blends tell how much seed to apply per acre. This information is found on the bag. Follow the manufacturer's recommendations. It's tempting to exceed the recommended level, because if one bag is good, two must be better, right? Dead wrong! If you apply too much seed, the now overcrowded plants produce less forage per acre. On the other hand, don't try to stretch your dollars too far. Sow too few seeds and weeds will encroach between the plants. If you're confident in your soil and its preparation, plant as recommended. If you don't expect good germination or if deer density is high, plant a bit more.

High-quality seed can be expensive and your dollars will stretch further if you proceed carefully. If you don't have an expensive metered seeder - and most people don't - get a small, food-type scale to measure out a quarter-acre at a time and use an over-the-shoulder crank seeder about ($20) to spread it, they are very effective. Better to trickle your seed and go over the same quarter acre of ground a couple of times than to blow it out the first 20 yards (been there done that). Don't pour too much seed into the hopper all at once, especially if you're using a large-capacity seeder. Trust us, $100 of clover seed can disappear before you know it. If you're hand seeding 2.8 mph is the average walking speed. Some hand-held seeders cost less than $20.

If you are seeding by hand, get a buddy and a length of rope. Give the seeder a spin and have your helper take one end of the rope out to the end of the seed coverage. Walk parallel the length of the field, stop and pivot around your helper one rope length. The seeder is now one-half coverage width away from the helper. Reverse direction with your helper retracing his steps and you will get even seed coverage. Get your rope and buddy out in the field; don't worry, it only sounds complicated, and you will get the hang of it.

Using a buddy and a piece of rope will make the whole seeding process a lot easier. Most spreaders will throw seed about 20 feet, 10 feet on either side of the planter.

You might also want to consider using an ATV or tractor driven seeder. A three acre food plot is a lot of ground to seed by hand. The Cadillac of food plot seeders is called the Firminator™. It is wheel-driven, has a great seed take up and metered drop system, and it also hauls along its own disc and cultipacker.

Do not hand-cast the seed. This is wasteful and creates uneven stands. Hand-casting is for the movies.

Food plotters often hire local farmers to work their bigger food plots. These fellows have the equipment to get it done in a hurry. One word of caution, farmers often "drill" their seed into the ground. This works great with most grains but is not the right approach with food plot blends. Most blends contain five to eight plant varieties and are designed to be spread evenly across the ground not deposited in rows six to eight inches apart (drilling). Using a drill to plant blends in lines will crowd too many seeds into too little space. The seeds will be competing with each other in a way not intended by the manufacturer.

Also, do not hand-cast the seed. This is wasteful and creates uneven stands. Hand-casting is for the movies.

An acre is often difficult to judge in the field. In rough terms, a football field, which is 50 yards wide and 100 yards long, covers about one acre. Hand-held measuring wheels are useful for precise calculations. Laser range-finders designed for hunting are also great for laying out food plots, we use the them all the time. Now you have two excuses to buy one.

After seeding, run the cultipacker once over the food plot. A roller also works well. If you're planting clover, rape, chicory or other small seeds, don't bury them too deeply. They should be in the top quarter-inch of soil. Some people like to disk after seeding, but we don't. A disk usually puts tiny seeds too deep into the soil, causing most of the sprouts to die before they ever reach daylight. If you cannot "contact" the seed to the soil by rolling, we believe it's better to leave the job to Mother Nature. On tiny food plots, we sometimes "drive the seed in" with our Argo, which has balloon turf tires. ATV s work okay, but no sharp corners or hot-rodding. This is not a job for a teenager working without supervision.

Utilization Cages Tell the Story

After planting, place some utilization cages in your food plots. Make them from 1 x 2-inch welded wire, 3 feet in diameter and 3 feet tall. A 12-foot length of the wire mesh works nicely. Be sure to stake cages securely, because deer and other wildlife bump them. This tool helps you gauge how much the plot is being used, and indicates how many more plots you should plant; if any. If six weeks pass and you notice the food plots vegetation is 18 inches high inside the cage and 2 to 3 inches tall outside, you have high deer use.

This is good news and bad. The good news is the stuff is growing and deer love it. The bad news is that by winter, there won't be much left. You should look to plant more food plots or thin your herd dramatically. A deer will eat 1.5 tons of food per year, with much of that coming from food plots, assuming you have them. Paying attention to how intensively deer use food plots and browse areas reveals a lot about the herd and its needs.

Photo by Matt Harper

A "utilization cage" in each plot is a must. Cages tell you how much your plot is being used by feeding deer. Too much or too little use might mean problems. Twelve feet of 3-foot high welded wire and a wooden stake make a fine cage.

People touring our Demo Center are often surprised we don't grow much corn in our food plots. Why not? Honestly, we haven't had the room until lately. Corn is a one-month wonder in our region and does nothing for antler growth and body size. Unless you plant large tracts of it, it is gone before you know it. Other plants produce forage year round and give a much higher nutritional return per acre. Also, every farmer in our county plants corn. Some leave it standing all winter. As we expand our food plot acreage we expand our corn planting but green forages will always be our main staple.

We prefer a mixture of high-protein forages that stay available all year, from early spring through winter. We want to meet the nutritional needs of lactating does, nursing fawns and bucks grow-

By mid-May, our clovers are producing major tonnage, and are starting to get ahead of the deer herd. The chicory kicks in shortly after the clover, so by mid-June we're often knee-high in clover and chicory.

ing antlers. Clovers, chicories, brassicas and some alfalfas are hard to beat. We only plant name brand forages designed for deer. These blends grow low and dense, and are low in stem material (except brassicas stalks), or lignin. Their density keeps down competing weeds. They're designed to be grazed, and as such, mature at different times of the year. The Whitetail Institute of North America has been researching and developing deer forages since 1988. We recommend you use only name brand forages, they save you huge amounts of money and time and your deer will thrive on them.

We don't plant cattle forages like red clover, tall white ladino clover, timothy grass. Cattle forages like these are grown to be chopped or baled and fed dry. They are high in coarse stem materials and lignin, which deer do not digest as well as cattle do. We call clovers that grow hip-high on fibrous stems "feel good" clovers. You feel good when you walk by the stand because of its height and appearance, but that's about the end of it. "Stemmy" for-

Photo by Charles J. Alsheimer

This band of bucks is chowing down after a long difficult breeding season. They're in the process of regaining the weight they lost during the rut. This is why we call brassicas the secret weapon of Northern food plots.

ages grow that high because deer don't care to eat them when more digestible cultivars are growing nearby.

A food plot program should have some food plots or fields dedicated to producing tons of nutrition. Done correctly, these plots should produce nutritious forage year round, even in the North. On the Demo Center, spring green-up starts in mid-April. Our clover blends kick in then and are heavily used by pregnant does. By mid-May, all of our clovers are producing major tonnage, and are starting to get ahead of the herd. The chicory kicks in shortly after the clover, so by mid-June, we're often knee-high in clover and chicory.

We then begin a mowing program to control weeds and keep the plots fresh. We mow the top one-third of the plants when they reach about 12 inches tall. During the growing season, we can mow on a Saturday and by the next Wednesday; the plot looks like it never saw a mower. We mow all summer to control weeds and keep our plots fresh. Early season mowing stimulates clover and chicory and results in increased tonnage grown. It also keeps weeds out of your plots.

The only time we don't mow is during dry spells. Speaking of dry spells, chicory is the secret weapon for dry conditions. It has an incredibly long taproot, which allows it to thrive in drought-like conditions. In 2002, (2005 wasn't much better) we endured the second driest summer in New York history, and our clovers resembled toast for 45 days. Chicory thrived the entire time.

The only trouble was, by the end of the drought, we could barely find a chicory plant on the place. The deer had mowed almost every one of them to the ground. Even so, they kept growing and reappeared when the clover came back with the rain. When the deer zeroed in again on the clover, the chicory got its chance to thrive once more.

We plant brassicas which carries over into the winter and is pretty much cleaned up by March. The Whitetail Institute calls their brassicas product "Winter-Greens " due to its winter feeding capability. This leaves the deer about a month or two to make a living without our help. We notice our deer hanging around south facing springs and seeps during early spring, taking advantage of nature's earliest green-up.

Feeding food plots are important to our program. Our harvested deer have increased in weight about 20 percent from the time we started weighing them in the early 1990s, their racks are noticeably larger, too. No deer management program is complete without thinking about year round nutrition. Therein lies the beauty of serious food plots.

Photo by Charles J. Alsheimer

Chapter X

Food Plots for Hunting

You have left the NorthCountry tram and are walking down a winding 6-foot-wide path that opens into a half-acre clearing. This field is carpeted in rich, ankle deep, brassicas and clover. This clearing has an irregular shape, with several hunter-hiding pines on the fringe. Man-made licking branches have been strategically placed within bow range of two well-hidden tree stands. The brush piles ensure no buck can get downwind of a hunter during a prevailing westerly wind.

The stage is set for success. But a year before, this setup was just another half-acre of brush and cover. It was part of an 80-acre overgrown pasture and almost impossible to hunt because of its density.

Hunting food plots are laid out differently than feeding plots. They're usually smaller -¼ to ¾ acres - irregularly shaped, and planted to attract deer during the hunting season. Cover juts into the plot to take advantage of wind direction and maximize hunter concealment. These peninsulas of cover provide close-range encounters for hunters, and add visual interest to the plot. Good hunting plots look like they've been there forever because they blend into the landscape. While feeding plots are laid out for agricultural efficiency, hunting plots are set up for close encounters with game.

Take Your Time Laying it Out

Before creating and setting up a hunting plot, it's vital to select your hunting location. Analyze how deer move in and out of the area by studying their trails. Early spring is a good time for this. Consider prevailing winds during the hunting season, and leave concealment cover intact. Consider bedding areas and anticipate a deer's route from the bedding area to the plot area. Study wind factors and weather patterns the hunting season before you lay out your plot. In our location, prevailing winds come from the west, varying southwest to northwest. We set up most of our plots to take advantage of these winds. Spend time at these sites with wind

Deer love edge environments with their assortments of cover and foods. Good hunting plots have irregular edges, with scrapes and licking branches within easy range of the stand.

152

Before starting bulldozer or brushhog work, carefully lay out the plot's shape and size. Plan where to pile up the brush beforehand to make plot construction easier. The piled brush should be "hidden" and used to channel deer movement.

directional tools, such as Windfloaters™ from API Treestands. These little tufts of milkweed-like material are great for studying wind currents. Be sure to release them from tree-stand height. Better yet, release them from the tree you wish to hunt from. Smoke bombs work well, too, as do some light powders. Besides testing prevailing winds, it's also important to understand how morning and evening thermal drafts affect drifting scents.

Pay attention to how you approach your hunting plot. Deer usually try to approach smaller food plots with the wind in their face, but deer-blocking wind-rows created by felled trees and piled brush channel deer through ambush sites. We always try to use wind-rows of piled brush to prevent deer from entering the plot downwind of a bow stand. Wind-rows get there with the help of a bulldozer or chainsaw.

Once you've studied the area, begin laying out the location and shape of your plot, and where you'll place your stands. Whenever possible, locate your stands in dense, dark trees. Conifers are excellent hunting trees because they provide concealment and shelter from the elements.

Enclosed tower stands are weatherproof, and can accommodate heaters. Be sure they can hold two people. A comfortable enclosed stand is an ideal way to hunt with a beginner or friend.

Choosing a Stand

When good hiding trees are unavailable, some hunters prefer an enclosed tower stand. These stands can be particularly effective for gun-hunters, and when no suitable trees are available and ground hunting is impractical. Tower stands can be bought or made from 4 x 4 posts, plywood and 2 x 4s. Enclosed blinds like these are weatherproof, and can accommodate heaters. They're extremely comfortable. Be sure the stand can hold two people, because this is an ideal way to hunt with a beginner or good friend.

On the other hand, enclosed tower stands tend to be permanent and somewhat obtrusive. Mature deer on our property tend to give them wide birth even though they are seldom hunted. Tuck them away in the edge of the plot so they don't stick out like a sore thumb. Use trees and brush to disguise the silhouette. It will look more natural if it's camouflaged. For a year-round camo blind, go to a rural dump right after Christmas and look for artificial Christmas trees. Collect the Christmas-tree boughs and recycle them by attaching them to the sides of the box or blind. These synthetic evergreen boughs last for years and make the stand look like an evergreen clump. They can make your blind become one with the surrounding cover.

The most common stands are hang-ons, ladder-stands and, of course, climbers. Be sure not to cut down trees in strategic locations that will support or hide your tree stands. We don't build permanent stands into trees. They not only damage trees and are unsightly, but mature deer learn their whereabouts and avoid them. They are also unsafe in a couple of years. Check the wind 12 to 16 feet up in these trees with Windfloaters™. Two or three tree stands per plot are not too many. Each should be set up for a different wind direction. Set them early in the year and be selective about removing limbs that aid concealment. Craig likes clear shooting and always cuts off too many limbs. As a result, he often gets "made" by wary deer. Neil, on the other hand, being more agile and easi-

This hunter is about to experience the benefits of hunting over food plots.

er to hide, prunes little and blends in with the tree he's hunting in. Once you cut limbs, they're gone forever unless you're handy with bailing wire and limb loppers.

Don't forget ground-blind strategies. When no trees are suitable for hunting, and ground blinds are your only option, lay out the plot with that in mind. At other times, a ground blind can be a backup or strategic choice that is used perhaps once a year to ambush a buck that's wary of your tree-stand locations. Be creative when laying out the food plot, and plan multiple ambush sites so you can hunt in various winds. On some hunting plots, wind conditions

Food plots designed for hunting attract deer at all times of the day because they often bed within yards of the plots. Always sneak in and out, and don't be afraid to hunt them at odd times of the day.

might not be appropriate for certain stands and - based on which days you're able to hunt - you might have to avoid them for two or three years. Don't force the issue. Wait until you get the perfect wind to move in and kill that trophy whitetail!

Once a chainsaw or bulldozer removes a piece of cover, it will never be there again. Plan carefully. Plan in advance. Pick sites for your plots with hunting in mind. Hunting plots are often laid out in a wooded or heavy-brush environment. A bulldozer is usually needed to clear the ground. When using a moderate-sized bulldozer, plan on at least eight hours of bulldozer work per acre of ground to be cleared. Lighter brush can be mowed with a stout rotary mower and 30 hp tractor. Mowing and liming the brushed area for a couple of years takes care of all of the brush and improves your soil. Plant food-plot quality forage the second or third year, and you will have a killer plot.

This nasty, dirt-packed brush should not be left in a "halo" around the plot. Push it into one or two corridors as far from the plot as possible. You don't want to sit in a stand staring at ugly brush all day. Hide your trash. Your goal is to create a plot that looks like it's 5 years old just one month after it's planted.

Create Good-Looking Plots

Aesthetics should be considered in creating all food plots. After all, you will spend hours in those locations, and most of us would rather be surrounded by beauty than something that resembles a construction site. A skilled bulldozer operator can hide debris by pushing it into the brush on a diagonal line to the plot. Initially, you

> *Aesthetics should be considered in creating food plots. After all, you will spend hours in those locations, and most of us would rather be surrounded by beauty than something that resembles a construction site.*

should push the brush pile at least 30 yards from the plot's edge. That way it won't back up into the edge of the plot. Clearing debris is nasty work, and it's tempting to leave several piles around the edges. It takes more work, but we suggest creating no more than two piles, and hiding those piles by pushing them as far from the plot as possible. A bulldozer operator unfamiliar with food-plot conditions will want to leave all debris banked around the food plot like a halo. This is ugly, and it blocks the deer's entrance and exit trails. Tell the bulldozer operator what you want beforehand so he can lay it out. A month after its construction, a food plot should look like it has been there for five years. Paying attention to details now reaps dividends as you sit hour after hour watching the plot.

As a bowhunter, you must be on high alert when hunting small food plots. If you wait for deer to enter the plot before drawing your bow, it might be too late. They might hear you or catch your movement. During the 2001 rut, we knew some quality bucks were working near a small hunting plot. Craig was in his stand 20 minutes when he heard a deer marching along a trail that paralleled a

This hunting plot was built two weeks before this photo was taken. It is irregularly shaped. Hunting trees still stand along its edges. The brush has been hidden, and the plot is simply beautiful.

food plot. As expected, the deer met a wind-row and followed it into the field. Craig suspected it was a buck, but waited for it to enter the field before grabbing his bow. Before Craig could react, the 120-class buck was 15 yards away, and bowhunter and quarry were face to face. Craig managed to get his bow and draw it slowly, but just as he was aligning his pin and peep sight, the deer snorted and ran. This was an amateur performance by someone who knows better than to get caught flat-footed with the bow on its hanger! Be alert and get your bow ready as soon as you suspect deer.

Neil's Now- Famous Plots

Over the years, Neil has sited dozens of hunting food plots. He has also studied which types of plot layouts work well for bowhunting, and which don't quite cut it. Remember, the purpose of a hunting plot is to attract and kill deer, not just attract and feed them. Neil has taken small hunting-plot designs to another level of mastery, and developed a series of plots we call Neil Dougherty's Signature Plots. They have been written about in magazines and featured on TV. These layouts have produced dozens of deer over the years, and at least one of these designs should work in almost any hunting food-plot setting you have on your property.

It's important to note we do not recommend round food plots. We can't think of one application where a round plot is the ticket. They're difficult to plant, and do little to control deer movements. Round works in fish bowls, but not in hunting food plots. Square plots aren't much better.

Before tackling a hunting plot, take time to study the wind, the lay of the land, and deer-movement patterns. Next, study the following diagrams and utilization criteria to determine which setups would work best for you on your property. Duplicating one or more of these designs will pay dividends when that trophy of a lifetime pays a visit.

Food plots are usually sited in one of two ways. Sometimes you create your own plots from relatively uniform cover, and sometimes you use existing open spaces created by farming. The first three plots we describe on the following pages fit the former category and allow you to maximize creativity. However, they require serious equipment for clearing brush. At the minimum, a stout rotary mower is required. More than likely, you will also need a bulldozer.

Neil's See-Through Hourglass Food Plot©

This plot is probably Neil's favorite design. It is also seems to be the most popular design with food plot enthusiasts. The Hourglass plot's unique design allows you to create a larger-than-

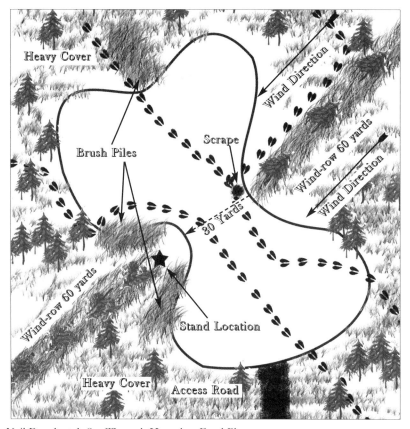

Neil Dougherty's See-Through Hourglass Food Plot   ©*NorthCountry Whitetails LLC 2002*

160

normal bowhunting food plot. Although most bowhunting food plots should be less than a half-acre in size, the Hourglass can cover up to an acre. Planted with a mix of fall attractants it is deadly.

The key to Neil's See-Through Hourglass design is its neck that is about 30 yards wide. This is where your stand should be located. Two stands can be placed there to take advantage of different winds. Licking branches and mock scrapes should also be located in the neck. It's important that deer be able to see that the neck doesn't dead-end. That is, deer should be able to see some open

The food plot's neck serves as a stopping place for most deer. Not only does it have a scrape and licking branch, but the neck also affords deer their best visibility of the entire plot

space beyond the neck, no matter where they are on the plot. This piques their curiosity and draws them into the neck to see what lies beyond.

The neck of the food plot will serve as a stopping place for most deer. Not only because of the signposts - the scrape and licking branch - you placed there, but because the neck affords deer their best visibility of the entire plot. Deer relax more when they can see what's ahead as well as behind.

Keep deer from approaching behind your stand by blocking that direction with brush-piled wind-rows. Deer will learn to approach the plot from another direction. Wind-rows should also be used on the upwind side to direct the deer's approach.

Locating the Hourglass plot in thick cover increases deer visitations during hunting hours. Mature bucks spend most of their daylight hours in thick cover, but will visit this plot for a quick mouthful of food or to check for does.

Neil's Boomerang Bushwhack Plot©

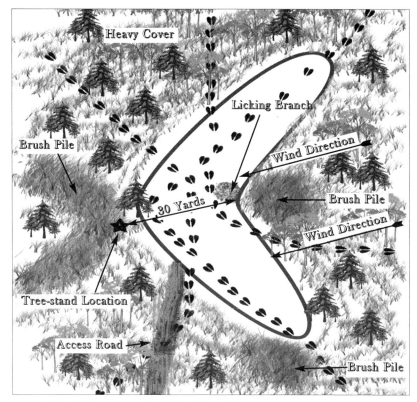

Neil Dougherty's Boomerang Bushwhack Food Plot   ©NorthCountry Whitetails LLC 2002

Neil's Boomerang Bushwhack food plot adapts better to smaller areas than the Hourglass plot. In particular, it works in narrower bands of cover, and generally covers a half-acre or less when set up for bowhunting. It's often planted with an annual fall attractant with planting timed to reach peak palatability during the hunting season.

The key to the Boomerang is the plot's ability to intercept multiple deer trails, and once deer enter the plot, to draw them through the elbow. The draw occurs because the gentle curve of the elbow reveals additional open space with each step the deer takes. Deer do not see the far end of the Boomerang until they're in the elbow's curve.

Like the Hourglass, the Boomerang is best located in thick, brushy areas.

Neil's Long-Shot "S"©

Another versatile plot that can be created in thick cover is Neil's Long-Shot "S" food plot. This plot works well for bow or gun hunters because it allows gun hunters to spot deer at longer ranges while concentrating deer in one easy to hunt location for bowhunters. It is especially effective when located in funnels and crossings. It also allows you to hunt long, narrow strips of brush, which are often found in farm country.

A Long-Shot "S" food plot is about 20 yards wide, and its length is determined by topography and the maximum distance

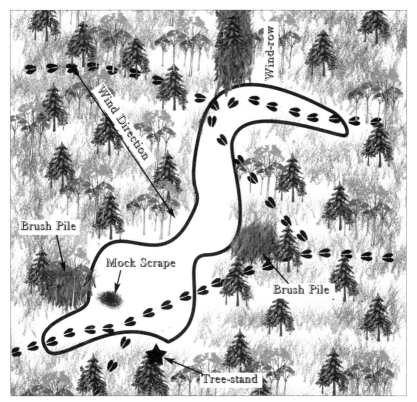

Neil Dougherty's Long Shot "S" Food Plot   *©NorthCountry Whitetails LLC 2002*

you'll shoot. Its distinctive feature is a bulge somewhere on the "S". The bulge is about 30 yards wide in the spot where you bowhunt. It features licking branches, mock scrapes and deer-blocking brush piles downwind of the stand. The bulge will encourage deer to congregate and linger and it's also the spot that cruising bucks are sure to check out.

Even though this plot is long and stretches conveniently from Point A to Point B, don't use it as your transportation route. Human traffic on this food plot will ruin it for hunting in a hurry. This plot is best planted with long-lasting perennials like clover and chicory because its irregular shape makes cultivation difficult.

More Designs

Topography often dictates food-plot design. This is especially true in farm country, which is often checker boarded with squares and rectangles of alternating woods and fields, with an occasional brush-lot thrown in for good measure. Straight edges and right angles are everywhere, as are abrupt transitions between cover types.

The food plots described in the next few pages take advantage of topographical features and as such are relatively easy to build.

Neil's Strip Stake-Out Food Plot©

Neil's Strip Stake-Out plots follow the topography, especially existing woods and thick cover. They're very effective when used as a food source between woods and fields or woods and brush. For these plots, you create a long, narrow, about 35 x 75 yards-strip adjoining an area where deer are comfortable, like a woods or brushy area. The trick is to get deer to enter the strip where you can get a bowshot. The area you have "staked out". The key is what you plant and when you plant it.

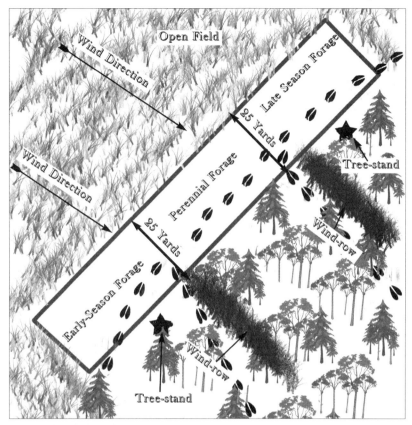

Neil Dougherty's Strip Stake-Out Food Plot   ©*NorthCountry Whitetails LLC 2002*

Study access trails and manipulate which trails will be using log or brushy windrows. Woodlots adjoining fields often have wire fences where the woods meet the field. Look for gaps in the fence as likely places for deer to cross. If the fence has too many gaps, consider fixing it. Plant forages with an eye toward peak palatability, which pays huge benefits. Knowing which forages deer prefer during different phases of the hunting season help you determine stand sites ("stake outs").

Good shooting is often at 30 to 50 yards back into the cover, because mature bucks often scent-check the plot downwind from inside the cover. Get downwind of his scent-check trail and you'll have him. Don't over-hunt these types of plots, because deer quickly learn to shy away from tree-stand setups along field edges. Climbing stands work well for these setups.

Neil's Corner Converger Food Plot©

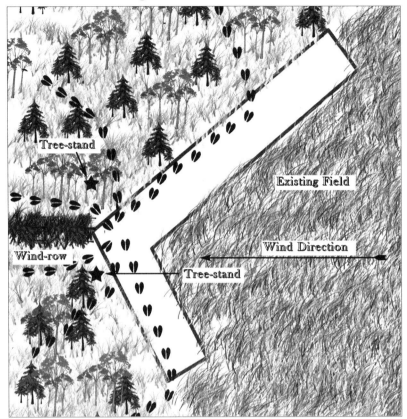

Neil Dougherty's Corner Converger Food Plot   *©NorthCountry Whitetails LLC 2002*

Corners where different covers meet have always been deer hotspots. They really heat up when planted with food-plot forages. The Corner Converger design makes the inside corners of fields hunting hotspots by concentrating deer. This design should not exceed 70 yards on the long leg and 30 yards on the short leg. The width should not exceed 25 yards. Sunlight-shading branches that overhang the food plot should be trimmed before planting.

A plot like this can be built with an ATV in about 4-6 hours per half acre and a disc. Be sure to spray the area you want to plant with a glyphosate-based herbicide a couple of weeks before working the soil. Extra tough, sod-bound areas might need to be sprayed in the fall and sprayed again in the spring before working in order to get a good seed bed for planting. Weighing the ATV and disc down with old feed bags filled with sand or soil is helpful when tackling sod ground. Be sure you don't work your machine too hard.

One key to this plot is a wind-row that extends into the woods or brush to channel deer into the corner. The second key is planting the plot with forages that achieve peak palatability during the hunting season. Ideally, the existing field's forages will have long lost their appeal to deer. A good example would be a food plot full of brassicas next to a farmer's alfalfa field. The brassicas becomes very attractive just as the alfalfa loses its appeal in cold weather. Bucks will check out the plot from the cover of the woods. But instead of skirting the plot, they will follow the wind-row into the corner ambush.

Neil's Comfortable Corner©

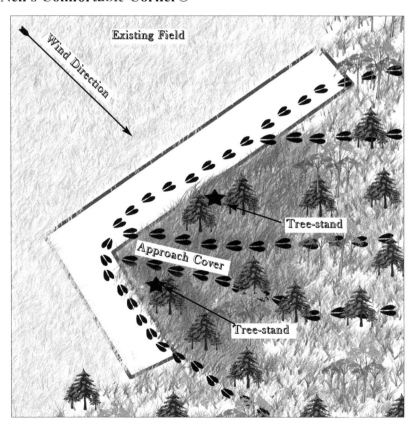

Neil Dougherty's Comfortable Corner Food Plot   *©NorthCountry Whitetails LLC 2002*

The Comfortable Corner is designed to concentrate deer on the cover side - usually a woodlot - of a food plot. Hunters have known for years that corners like this make good ambush sites as deer travel the edges of cover. The Comfortable Corner takes this to the next level by combining an attractive food source (the plot) with cover (brush, etc.). The cover is created in the corner where the woodlot and the plot meet, which contributes to the comfort factor. The food serves as an attractant.

To build a Comfortable Corner, you'll likely need to increase sunlight to the corner, and enrich the soil with lime and fertilizer. If you're working with a wooded corner, you'll probably need to remove about two-thirds of the overstory for about 50 yards in all directions. For that reason, be sure to choose your stand-trees first. The chainsaw work will regenerate brush and young trees, and the area will grow up with forbs, briars and other food and cover. Deer tend to stage in this area, and bump around in the brush while browsing before entering the plot. They will also seek this area as the safest way to enter the food plot. This makes an ideal bowhunting site. However, do not over-hunt it. Too much human contact quickly turns the corner from a comfortable corner to a corner to avoid.

How much hunting activity is too much? It's best to hunt such sites, at most, once or twice a week. Get in, get out, and give it plenty of rest. Over hunting eliminates daytime deer utilization. If deer detect your presence, they'll feed nocturnally. On evening hunts, try not to leave your stand when deer are still feeding in the plot. Even if it's dark, have someone pick you up on an ATV, which moves deer off the plot without overly alarming them.

Food Plots Should Work Together

Food plots should not be laid out in isolation on your property. That is, they should relate to each other. The accompanying diagram shows about 50 acres of cover and food plots. Notice how the

Boomerang and Hourglass hunting plots relate to the large destination food plots and bedding areas. Note also how smaller hunting plots relate to each other, and how one works in a north-northwest wind, and the other works in a south-southwest wind. Plan your layouts carefully, both from macro (overall property) and micro (individual plots) levels.

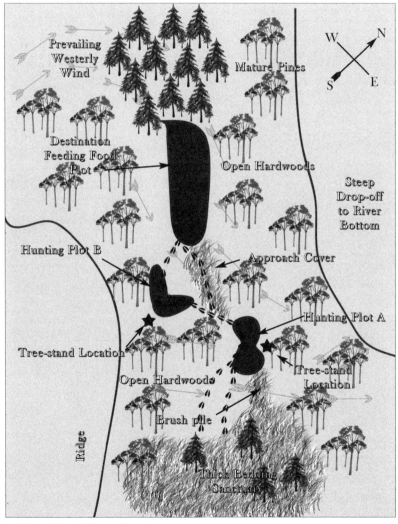

Food Plots Should Work Together   ©*NorthCountry Whitetails LLC 2002*

Plantings

While perennials are great for feeding plots, annuals come into their own as hunting plots. We like to plant hunting plots with annuals that are designed to offer peak palatability when we want to hunt over them. This usually works on properties where deer numbers are in line with food sources but small plantings of tender young annuals can be totally wiped out if too many deer key in on them at one time.

We normally plant in mid-August to mid-September. We like a mix of wheat, oats, clovers and brassicas - for bow season, which runs mid-October to mid-November. And we rely heavily on brassicas, for late season (Nov-Dec). Clover patches work well at either time, but in our area, they're best planted in spring. It's possible to plant fast growing annual covers for fall hunting plots, but perennial fall clover plantings won't come into their own until the

Photo by Charles J. Alsheimer

This big guy will be in and out of this small hunting plot in no time. During the rut, chances are he won't even stop to eat. Be ready before he shows because you won't get a second chance.

next year. A good stand of brassicas planted in spring also makes a terrific hunting plot come late fall.

The Whitetail Institute's Winter Greens™ product is a nice pure brassicas blend that can be mixed with winter hardy wheat or oats for a fall planting. Sow wheat and oats at 100lbs. per acre and Winter Greens™ according to the manufacturers recommendations, 6 lbs. per acre.

Hunting food plots are great places to spend time. We have spent hundreds of hours in and over them, and never tire of the up-close, personal encounters they provide with deer and other wildlife. Lay them out carefully, plant them with cultivars deer prefer during the hunting season, and you'll experience deer hunting like you've never known before.

We promise!

Chapter XI

Planting by the Compass

The tram pulls up to a sun scorched food plot on the top of the hill. It's July and the clover growing there is already shut down for the summer. No deer are to be found. They haven't used this plot in three weeks. They have gone elsewhere. Thankfully the else-where is just over the hill on the north slope. Our clover plots on that side of the mountain are doing just fine. They are still moist and producing beautifully on their sun-sheltered slopes.

Creating a successful food plot is similar to building a solid foundation under a house. Even the best food plot blends can't grow properly without a solid foundation. There are numerous factors that contribute to the overall food plot foundation. Soil tests performed by a professional lab will assess pH level and nutrients. Once that is done, it's relatively simple to amend the soil with lime and fertilizer to build a proper growing foundation. But, due to the relative small size of food plots other factors are at play. Plot location and weather conditions can make or break a food plot season. Many farmers plant by the moon; we plant food plots by the compass - here's why.

Soil Moisture-Angle of the Sun

Neil has assisted hundreds of landowners with challenging planting conditions over the years and has found that one of the greatest struggles land managers face is controlling soil moisture. There are several key factors that contribute to soil moisture loss. Sunlight, soil type, wind and planting techniques are among the top factors that contribute to moisture loss.

The greatest factor in the battle for soil moisture conservation is direct sunlight. The sun is necessary for all growth within food plots; however; too much sun is not a good thing. This is especially true for food plots that are planted in the traditionally dry areas of the Carolina's and deep south. To understand the impact of the sun on the plants in your food plots just follow the sun as it makes its daily journey across the sky.

Imagine a hunting food plot located in the woods and surrounded by mature trees on all sides. The morning sun rises in the east,

Direct sunlight can rob soil of critical moisture limiting the production of even the toughest plants. This dry clay soil has baked and split under the hot summer sun.

as the morning progresses and the angle of the sun increases, sunlight will start to beam into the western portion of the food plot. The plants on the western side of the food plot are absorbing early-morning life-giving sunlight. Cool temperatures combined with dew on the tender plants allow the plot to absorb the sunlight without losing critical soil moisture.

As the sun continues to rise in the sky and midmorning approaches, the entire food plot is exposed to direct sunlight. At this time of the day, the dew has burned off and the air temperature is increasing. Warmer temperatures combined with direct sunlight start to pull moisture out of both the ground

Tall trees on the left (west) side of the field shades up to 50% of this plot offering late afternoon protection from the sun. This is a factor in small food plots, not in large agricultural fields

and the plants growing within the field. The entire field is experiencing the negative impact of a hot dry day.

As the sun continues to move across its arc and the daytime temperatures reach their peak, soil moisture loss within the field is at its highest rate. Typically, the hottest time during a summer day is around four in the afternoon. The sun is located in the western portion of the sky. At this time of the day, sunlight is beaming directly onto the eastern portion of the food plot while the western side of the food plot enjoys the shade offered by the tree edge. During a cool wet year the east side of the plot will flourish. The west side will do better than the east during a droughty year.

An overall understanding of the arc of the sun and its impact on soil moisture will enhance your ability to create high-quality food plots. For example, if you're planting in a soil type that typically dries out during the summer, such as sandy soils, it's a good idea to use tall trees to block afternoon sun. Blocking afternoon sun will allow the sandy soil to hold more moisture and produce better quality plants. Conversely, if you suspect your ground is too wet you can use the sun to dry the planting site. In wet sites be sure that trees do not block the afternoon sun; promoting more soil moisture loss, and help dry the ground when your food plots are planted.

The angle of the ground works in conjunction with the angle of the sun to impact the amount of soil moisture retained within the food plot. This is especially true for those of us with hilly food plot locations. The deflection or absorption of the sunlight will contribute to either cooler or higher soil temperatures. Think back to sixth grade Earth science. Remember the experiment where the sun was represented by a flashlight and the earth by a basketball? The

In Northern rolling terrain, it's important to understand the direction of the roll. Northern slopes face away from the sun (cool and moist). Southern facing plots receive more direct sunlight (warm and dry). A plot's aspect to the sun influences growing conditions at different times of the year as well as deer behavior.

warmest portions of the earth are located along the equator where the sunlight is absorbed at the most direct angle. The farther away one gets from the equator the more indirect the light and the cooler the temperatures. In food plots the angle of the sunlight works in similar ways especially on sloped ground.

In a food plot if the ground slope faces south, less sunlight is deflected off the surface of plot and the ground temperature increases as it takes a direct hit from the sun. Although the soil temperature increase may only be a few degrees on a sunny day it dramatically alters growth potential of plants. It is most noticeable in food plots where the ground slope faces south but also rolls around to face north. The temperature difference on a given day can be 3-4 degrees. In this scenario during the hot dry month of July, forages may go dormant on the south-facing slope but remain productive on the north-facing slope.

"In a food plot if the ground slope faces south, less sunlight is deflected off the surface of plot and the ground temperature increases as it takes a direct hit from the sun."

North, South, East and West

In the north, a southwestern slope will absorb sunlight during the afternoon when the daytime temperatures are at their peak. Southwestern exposures experience the warmest soil temperatures and lose soil moisture at the quickest rate. Forages on southwestern slopes typically struggle during hot dry summer months. A northwestern slope reflects the vast majority of the sunlight during the daytime, only absorbing sunlight during the afternoon hours. A northwestern slope typically will have moderate soil temperatures with a moderate level of soil moisture loss; expect this site to do

Aerial photos like this coupled with topo maps, are great for locating directional slopes. When laying out the plot be sure to check the slope's aspect to the sun with a compass.

well during most summers. A northeast-facing slope will absorb sunlight during the morning hours when the air temperature is cool. This site will retain high levels of soil moisture, and typically perform extremely well in hot dry summers. A southeastern-facing slope will experience a quick warm up in the morning, as early-morning rays of sunshine are absorbed within the soil. Southeastern facing slopes are typically excellent planting locations; they warm up quickly in the morning, but reflect the afternoon sun and remain cool. This promotes soil moisture conservation and increased plant growth.

A balanced approach is required in order to have consistent food plot success year after year. On our Demo Center some summers are extremely wet, our south facing plots expel the soil moisture and perform well on dry years. On the other hand, the north facing food plots remain too cool and wet and plant production is limited. On dry years, the south facing slopes may go dormant during the hottest and driest summer months, while the north facing slopes remain productive feeding our deer. If you plant by the compass you have a much better chance of producing quality food plots, regardless if it's a dry or wet year.

Hunt the Sun

The angle of the sun also can impact the plots when it comes to hunting season. As a general rule of thumb deer will be drawn to plots that are producing the highest quality forage. If you've just passed through a dry summer it's a good bet that your deer will be feeding heavily on the north facing food plots during the first stages of the hunting season. On the other hand, if it has been a very wet year, the south facing food plots will be producing more and better forages during the first stages of the hunting season. As the temperature drops during the fall, switch your hunting tactics and concentrate on areas where the soil temperature remains high. Whether these areas are

The angle of the sun combined with the duration of direct sunlight, affects the soil temperature and soil moisture level within plots. Use a meat thermometer or soil temperature guage to check your ground temperatures.

food plots or not, more growth can be found in areas with higher soil temperatures. Perhaps the best way to think about your property is to envision the areas of ground slope as grocery stores. As the air temperature cools some of the grocery stores start to close for the year. By the end of the hunting season the stores remaining open are the ones to maintain the highest soil temperature typically facing southwest.

Neil's favorite hunting food plots always seem to face south. The reason for this is the angle of the sun which warms the ground and increases the amount of plant growth late in the fall. Sometime during bow season the soil temperature on our north facing plots drops

---

Southwestern facing food plots become deadly weapons during the later portion of the fall hunting season as deer are forced to follow plant growth within food plots.

---

below the minimum requirements for plant growth. These food plots quickly go dormant and our deer pull off them. A southwestern facing food plot absorbs sunlight and maintains a higher temperature range, and often continues to produce forage for an additional few weeks. Southwestern facing food plots become deadly weapons during the later portion of the fall hunting season as deer are forced to follow plant growth within food plots. Deer also seek out the warmer temperatures found on these slopes.

Additional Moisture Robbers

The impact of the sun is by far the greatest contributing factor to soil moisture within the planting site, however there are a few other factors that are worth mentioning. Hilltop food plots that experience lots of wind are also typically drought areas. The increased airflow over the plants increases the amount of moisture loss within plants and decreases their drought tolerance. Hilltops are typically tough on food plots. Conversely, plots sheltered from the wind typically do well.

In addition to the sun and the wind, improper planting techniques often are to blame for poor plant performance. If you're managing property in the traditionally dry areas of the country, pay special attention to planting techniques that conserve soil moisture. One of the easiest ways to conserve soil moisture is to use an herbicide to kill the existing plant growth and then use a no-till drill to deposit the seed within the soil. The layer of dead grasses and thatch combined with a well-packed soil will retain the maximum amount of soil moisture.

Every time a plow or disk is used to break the integrity of the soil, moisture is lost. Perhaps the worst offender in the game for conserving soil moisture is a rototiller. One pass with a tiller and

"If you're managing property in the traditionally dry areas of the country, pay special attention to planting techniques that conserve soil moisture."

the soil has been loosened to the point where most of the soil moisture will quickly evaporate. The tiller is a great tool when it comes to planting food plots but should be used with caution in areas with a limited amount of rainfall.

One of the most useful techniques used to conserve soil moisture is a cultipacker. A cultipacker will compress the soil and eliminate air pockets. This will lead to increased soil moisture retention. Recently while planting on the research facility, Neil tried to take a shortcut after tilling a food plot. To save time, Neil broadcasted seed and made one pass with a cultipacker to bury the seed. As he inspected his work, he noticed that the ground was still fluffy, his feet sank into the soil about an inch when he walked over the prepared ground. Normally, rainfall would settle the soil and finish the packing job. However, this particular year turned out to be a dry year. Forty-five days after planting, only about 30% of the seed had germinated within the field, while weeds and grasses were

When it comes to planting food plots, the tiller is a great tool. However, you should use caution in areas with a limited amount of rainfall. Packing soil after tilling is generally a good idea.

everywhere. As Neil walked over the field, he noticed that the soil was still spongy under his feet. Using a shovel he made a cut in the soil and found that soil moisture was present 6-8 " within the ground, but was non existent in the top 2 inches of the fluffy tilled soil. To fix the problem he broadcast new seed over the field, and again cultipacked the ground. Two weeks later the field was lush and green with clover and chicory growing everywhere. The ground was no longer spongy under his feet, soil moisture from deep within the ground had made its way to up to the surface of the food plot and had germinated the seeds.

Properly maintaining soil moisture within the field will greatly reduce the competition of weeds. If you are routinely planting your field and experiencing high levels of weed growth, the first step should be to evaluate your planting practices and look for ways to conserve soil moisture.

Old time farmers are almost as fond of talking about their ground as they are of talking about the weather; It's their living. Deer depend on ground and weather to make their living as well. Planting food plots by the compass enables us to hedge our ground and weather bets. If one location fails, chances are another will prosper. Planting by the compass will keep your deer on your property throughout the year and have them where you want them when hunting season rolls along.

Chapter XII

Big Toys for Big Boys (and Girls)

The NorthCountry tram pulls into a large food plot. On your right is a row of well-used farm implements: plows, disks, spreaders, sprayers and a cultipacker. These are the serious tools of the food plot trade. To your left rests sample bags of lime and fertilizer. A soil sampling probe leans against the bags, further evidence of serious agricultural practices. Six half-acre test plots stretch before you, including this year's cafeteria style food plot, where some 75 experimental cultivars are being tested. You have entered one of NorthCountry Whitetail's research plots. Ten years before, we knew virtually nothing about agricultural practices. In fact, we didn't know a disk from a drag. But thanks to some local farmer friends, Neil's natural mechanical aptitude, and some industry experts we've gotten pretty good with agricultural machinery. We even produced a DVD on it. If we can do it, you can too! This chapter will get you started.

Hunting food plots and small feeding food plots can be created with machines that range from simple hand tools to powerful tractors and plows. The same equipment that farmers use can be effective, but it's not mandatory, especially when you're just starting out. If you have a small area to work or are on a limited budget, you can still create food plots and attractive hunting spots. At its simplest, you can use a rake to rough up bare soil, spread some seed, and stamp it in with your feet. This procedure will take about a day for an eighth of an acre plot. This is as basic as it gets, but it works. There is no smell of fuel fumes, no noisy equipment, and nothing to break; except your back if you do more than a few hundred square feet. It's a good start, but if you're like most people, you'll soon graduate to more advanced methods.

ATVs for Small Plot Plantings

The next level of planting sophistication uses more serious equipment and a mechanized power source. This usually means ATV equipment, because most hunters own or can borrow an ATV.

ATV implements can be handy for planting logging roads and small clearings of one or two acres. An all-in-one implement saves time and labor by combining soil preparation, seeding and rolling in one pass. It's a serious piece of equipment.

Tough planting conditions require tough equipment. This eight-wheeled drive Argo has more than enough power and traction to pull even the heaviest ATV implements.

A variety of light-duty ATV attachments are available to help habitat managers create small food plots. ATVs are especially effective in remote, hard-to-reach areas or on small hunting plots like Neil's "Boomerang Bushwhack", the "See-Through Hourglass" or the "Long Shot "S" designs (see previous chapter).

If you are going to install food plots with an ATV you are going to need a machine with some guts. We like them to be at least 400ccs but 500 would be better and, it had better have 4 WD. We have a 750 that is a real performer but it is still a far reach from a tractor. Fortunately, most hunters buy 4WD general purpose utility machines, which if they have the guts will do a pretty good job. Those bright colored, high-backed screaming racing machines that we all love to hate are next to useless.

When it comes to implements, be careful. Some ATV implements work great, but others are little more than toys. It's important to consider the weight of the implement you're using, especially in tough soils where you need substantial weight to cut into the ground. Backyard garden implements that are designed to be pulled by a light-duty lawn tractor won't cut it. In addition, you need favorable soil conditions. Moist, but not wet, soils work up the best in most areas. Hard, sun-baked clay soil should be avoided at all costs, because it's almost impossible to work with a light weight implement.

We've had great success with some of the heavier duty pieces of equipment on the market. Our absolute favorite is the "Firminator™" by Modern Habitat Solutions. The Firminator is made in both a draw behind ATV and tractor model and it's first rate. It features an aggressive cutting disc, a world-class commercial grade seeder and a cultipacker all in one. It is quite heavy and needs about 500ccs out in front to get the job done.

If you have a 400cc or larger four-wheel-drive ATV, you can get a lot of work done, but it's unrealistic to expect to plant 4-and 5-acre fields with ATV implements. The amount of time required to

Although we own a 250-gallon sprayer with a 40-foot boom, we usually use this ATV sprayer. It's 25 gallon capacity will treat about one acre with herbicide or pesticides, but its value is its versatility and maneuverability. Its boomless sprayer makes it easy to maneuver in and out of tight spots, and transportation is a snap.

get the job done is much too great. Logging roads and ½ -to 1-acre fields are tailor made for ATV equipment. Plan on spending about four hours per ½-acre when using an ATV.

You might also consider a heavy-duty pull-behind mower if you have an ATV. Mowing brush and over-grown fields is an important part of creating habitat. ATV pull-behinds generally have their own gasoline engines. These mowers won't handle heavy brush, but they will cut trails and clearings in the weeds. Kunz Engineering makes some pretty nice looking models. They also have a nice line of ground preparation implements.

Bigger Toys - Tractors

If you're expecting to plant large feeding food plots, you'll need to step up a rung or two on the equipment ladder. For most situations, a 35- to 60-hp tractor is sufficient. We have been using a couple of shiny red Case-IH Farmalls® the past couple of years. These little beauties are just about perfect for food plot work. Ours have 4WD, which we cannot live without. They also feature front end loaders which are perfect for hauling seed, fertilizer, chemicals and a ton of other stuff around the property. They have had plenty of pull to handle our 6 and 8 foot tillage implements including a ground pulverizing 72-inch rototiller.

This handy 33-hp tractor is about right for serious food plot planting. It handles a 65" rototiller with ease, and doesn't groan when pulling a 6-foot Firminator. A bucket is super handy, and well worth the extra cost.

This 100-hp 4WD beauty is a bit of overkill for most food-plot work. Neil uses it in large feeding plots, where it makes quick work for any project, but we could get by without it. This is truly a big toy for big boys (and girls).

Best of all, at least as far as Craig is concerned, their controls operate like a street vehicle. That is, all of the dash levers, foot pedals, and instruments are set up pretty much like the vehicle you drive every day. Idiot proof. This might seem like no big deal until you get into a jam (which Craig often does) and you need to react quickly. You go on automatic reflex when things get a little tight and it's nice to be running a machine that goes there with you. Craig won't even run any of our old tractors with levers sticking out every which way. He knows his "weekend warrior" reflexes will go on automatic "street vehicle" just when he needs them most in a tight spot.

The next best thing, according to both Craig and Neil, is how easy these Cases are to hook up with implements. The lift arms and rest of the stuff behind the tractor have all kinds of adjustments to make disk and other implement hook up and adjustment a snap. No one likes crawling off and on a tractor trying to hook up implements. One time and you are pretty much done with these shiny red beauties.

You will also need a set of plows to go with the tractor. In fact, when preparing light soil or worked soil, a disk is often sufficient, and you won't need a plow. If you're shopping for plows, the rule of thumb is one bottom of plow for every 20 horsepower of tractor. Bottoms are the paddles that cut into the ground. After purchasing plows, you'll need a disk, a cultipacker or roller, and some way to spread seed. You'll also need a way to spray herbicide and, occasionally, pesticide. We have found the most practical way to spray Roundup® is with a small 25-gallon sprayer ($250) made for an ATV. About 25 gallons of fluid - one tank- will spray two acres. Although we have a 200-gallon tractor pull-behind commercial sprayer, we usually use the small four-wheeler model, because it's easier to handle.

Most of this equipment can be bought at auctions. The approximate costs are as follows: tractor, $2,000 to $6,000; plows, two or three bottom set, $275; an 8-foot disk, $525; 10-foot cultipacker, $650.

This Argo is one of the workhorses of our operation. We use it daily for dozens of projects, including seeding, hauling fertilizer and lime, cutting wood and, yes, transporting deer.

Photo by Whitetail Institute of North America

Herbicides save lots of ground preparation time by killing the weeds prior to cultivating. A herbicide is a must if you plan on using light duty ATV implements. Spray the field and wait one week for the chemical to do its work. Then turn the ground and plant. However, we prefer newer boomless sprayers.

Herbicides like Roundup®, Arrest™ and Slay™ can be very effective in saving time and controlling unwanted vegetation. We didn't use herbicides the first few years we had food plots. Previously, the process was to plow a field over, wait four or five days until the root systems and vegetation began to show again, and then disk the field, leveling the plowed ground. We would then wait two weeks for any living plants to regenerate and shoot back up. Then we would again disk and eliminate most of these weeds. All the time, we were using expensive fuel and compacting our already dense clay soil below while pulverizing the top few inches.

We would have a relatively weed-free food plot for a year or so until weeds and grasses appeared again. By the second year, we were mowing the plots to eliminate weeds. By the third or fourth year, we were about ready to start over again. That was just too much time and work for weekend warriors who had to travel 2 ½ hours to work their property. Using herbicides cuts the time dramatically, saves fuel, and avoids excessive soil compaction in clay-type soils. It also keeps weeds in check much longer.

During the late 1990s, we learned we could spray Roundup® one weekend - which took perhaps one hour - and then plow the food plot the next weekend, disk the next day, and then seed and plant. This amounted to two weekends worth of work and about four hours per acre. We spent only six hours per acre with the old method, but it dragged on for weeks. Because our property is located at a high elevation in the North, we must take advantage of spring soil moisture. As soon as the ground is ready to work, we need to get our seeds into the ground to get the most out of our relatively short growing season.

∙∙

With proper management and the selective
use of herbicides, we have extended the life
of our food plots to six years or more.

∙∙

Using herbicides allows us to seed earlier and take advantage of ideal planting conditions. With multiple food plots and limited time, we can't afford to drag out the work over an extended period.

After establishing a plot by starting with an herbicide kill, we do not see many weeds showing up until three or four years later. When grass begins to invade our plots, we use another herbicide, Arrest™, which eliminates grass, but does not kill broadleaf cultivars like chicory, brassicas and clover. Arrest™ keeps out the invading grasses and lets our broadleaf cultivars thrive. With proper management and the selective use of herbicides, we have extended the life of our food plots to six years or more. This is not to say we're crazy about herbicides. We only use them when necessary, which usually means one application per year. But we have evolved from abstaining skeptics to cautious believers. As a management tool, herbicides are effective and should be considered.

Another advantage of herbicides is that they allow you to practice "no-till" farming. When establishing new plots, no-till is highly recommended. In no-till agriculture, you skip the plowing and disking, and go straight to the seeding. No-till seeders cut narrow slits into the ground - or dead thatch that has been treated with an herbicide - with a blade-like hook, and deposit seeds into the slit. The slit closes automatically, and a week or so later green growth pops up in neat little rows in your food plots. Be careful not to bury small seeds too deep, no more than 1/4 of an inch.

No-till equipment has only one catch. It's very expensive. Because of its effectiveness and its relatively new presence in agriculture, you don't often see used no-till seeders for sale. But if money is no object, or you can hire a farmer who has one, no-till could be the way to go.

··

One or two passes with a 6- or 8-foot
wide rototiller will generally prepare even
the nastiest food plot for seeding.

··

Some food-plot enthusiasts have great success with heavy-duty rototillers behind their tractors. Once again, these are not the toys you see in backyard gardens. They're serious, heavy-duty implements carrying serious price tags.

One or two passes with a 70 in. wide rototiller will generally prepare even the nastiest food-plot for seeding. However, large rocks can wreak havoc with a rototiller, so if your soil has more rocks than dirt, find another alternative. We have found that you can prepare a one-acre plot with a 50hp tractor, a rototiller and plant it with The Firminator™ in 1.5 hours. The same tractor plowing (2 bottom), disking, and planting without the Firminator™ takes about 4 hours per acre.

It's easy to see why we like rototillers for food plots. One note of caution; rototillers are notorious "soil fluffers" and fluffy over-aerated soil does not hold and or transmit moisture well. Unless rain is on the way to compress the fluff, it's best to roll or cultipack the soil after rototilling and before seeding. They also till to a depth of about 6 inches. Years of tilling to a uniform depth while driving over the ground can lead to compressing the soil under the 6 inch depth. This creates what is called "hard pan". We break up the hard pan by plowing into it every five years or so.

The term "no-till" when applied to seed mixtures can be misleading. Read the directions and you will almost always see that some ground preparation is called for. Seeds don't grow without

··

Throwing expensive seed atop unprepared ground is like throwing your hard-earned money onto the same ground and just walking away.

··

making contact with dirt. It is that simple. Throwing a bunch of seeds on top of a layer of leaves or grass is a waste of time and money. We wish we didn't have to write this chapter and that you could wave the magic food-plot wand and have perfect plots every time. The reality of the food-plot business is that you'll almost always need mechanized equipment to get the job done.

We suggest you think through your equipment needs and seek the advice of an experienced farmer about what works best on your soil. Throwing expensive seed atop unprepared ground is like throwing your hard-earned money onto the same ground and just walking away.

Auctions and Roadside Sales

Unless you're smart about equipment, you must be careful at auctions. Fixing broken equipment is expensive and time-consuming. If you don't know what you're looking at, take an equipment expert with you. He will know what he's looking at and how much to pay. We've bought a few "bargain" pieces of equipment at roadside sales that have turned into overgrown rabbit shelters riddled with broken and twisted pieces of steel.

A good friend of ours gave a retired farmer friend an equipment wish list, a budget and a checkbook. The retired gentleman is happy to visit local auctions - and all farmers like auctions - because he has a goal and money to spend. This man knows his equipment and spends our friend's money like it's his own.

Whatever you do, don't buy junk. You need serviceable equipment. Junk equipment wastes your valuable time and money. You'll turn wrenches instead of planting, and worse, junky equipment can kill you. Early in our "farming career", Craig almost bought the farm when the brakes on an old bargain tractor let go, and he headed backward down a steep incline. He escaped injury but the scare was incredible. Two weeks later, a 50-hp tractor with almost-new shiny green and yellow paint replaced the death-trap. The newer tractor had given us perfect service for the 10 years leading up to this book.

Of course, no serious operation is complete without a PTO-driven rotary mower; also know as a brush-hog. These mowers vary from 5 feet wide to double batwings that can mow more than 20 feet of brush at a time. You must match your mower to your tractor because too much PTO horsepower can destroy a light duty mower. Conversely, too much mower can damage your tractor. In general, a 6-to 7-foot mower matches up pretty well with a 30-to 50-hp tractor.

Used equipment usually requires new owners to be handy with a wrench. Regular maintenance is a must with older equipment. Better to fix it in the shed than break it in the field.

You don't have to own a tractor and rotary mower to mow food plots. This ATV rotary mower by Kunz Engineering is a great rig for food plot mowing. It is tough yet agile. Best of all, you probably already own an ATV.

You can do tremendous amounts of habitat work with a rotary mower. Overly mature brush is made fresh again by mowing. Nasty, abandoned fields can be turned into deer feeding areas with mowing, liming, and a good dose of fertilizer. Lanes can be cut, and edge cover can be created with a routine mowing program. We mow brushy areas to ensure they're producing fresh cover and to keep them from maturing to the point where the overstory eliminates food and ground cover. Indeed, next to a chainsaw, a good rotary mower might be one of your most important purchases.

A well-equipped deer hunting property is generally a well-run operation. Although getting started is sometimes difficult, once you get on top of the equipment curve, it's relatively easy to stay there. Add equipment as your budget allows, and as your habitat-development program grows. Running good equipment can be fun. Working on broken junk all weekend when you should be planting is one of the most frustrating parts of habitat development. It drains energy and prevents you from achieving your goals. Regular maintenance of good, serviceable equipment helps you avoid this situation as much as possible.

Chapter XIII

Selecting Cultivars for the Food Plot

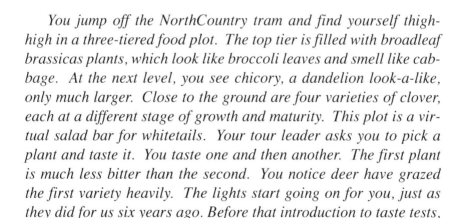

You jump off the NorthCountry tram and find yourself thigh-high in a three-tiered food plot. The top tier is filled with broadleaf brassicas plants, which look like broccoli leaves and smell like cabbage. At the next level, you see chicory, a dandelion look-a-like, only much larger. Close to the ground are four varieties of clover, each at a different stage of growth and maturity. This plot is a virtual salad bar for whitetails. Your tour leader asks you to pick a plant and taste it. You taste one and then another. The first plant is much less bitter than the second. You notice deer have grazed the first variety heavily. The lights start going on for you, just as they did for us six years ago. Before that introduction to taste tests, we knew little about peak palatability, whitetail nutrition and selecting forages.

A cultivar is a species planted for a specific purpose. In our case, the purpose is deer food. A "blend" is a number of cultivars planted together in a plot to provide variety.

Food plots remain important year-round. This lactating doe and her fawn need all of the spring/summer nutrition they can get. Getting this young buck off to a good start pays dividends in the months and years that follow.

When selecting cultivars for food plots, it's important to ask the question: "What do I want my food plots to contribute to the overall management program?" Do you just want something green to hunt over? If so, an annual cultivar planted during fall is usually green for hunting season and attracts deer. It won't be around next spring, but it will feed deer from late summer through fall. You might want to try a mixture of oats, wheat, and possibly brassicas.

Or, do you want cultivars that feed deer year-round, nourish lactating does and their fawns, and put pounds and antler inches on bucks? If so, you'll want a perennial food plot, which in the North is usually planted in spring, lasts four to five years if taken care of and produces highly nutritious forage from spring through fall. When it comes to year round feeding, clover is still king. Throw in some chicory or brassicas or both and you have a pretty powerful plot capable of producing three seasons of nutrition.

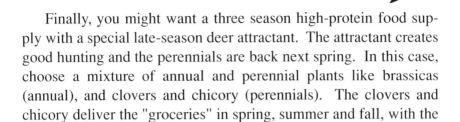

Finally, you might want a three season high-protein food supply with a special late-season deer attractant. The attractant creates good hunting and the perennials are back next spring. In this case, choose a mixture of annual and perennial plants like brassicas (annual), and clovers and chicory (perennials). The clovers and chicory deliver the "groceries" in spring, summer and fall, with the brassicas getting heavily eaten in fall and winter.

Many clovers shoot up quickly in early spring. By June they're knee high or taller. We call these "feel-good" clovers because you feel good when you see them growing. Unfortunately, they're not the best for deer.

By now you should be getting the idea. Different plants bring different attributes to the table (pun intended?). It's important to understand what plants bring what performance traits to your food plot program. Study cultivar options to understand how they perform in the field, and when deer are most likely to seek them out. Don't settle for an "if it's green, it's good" food plot philosophy.

We believe the goal of a serious food plot program is to feed deer with high quality forage for as many months as possible during the year. We also believe a good food plot program should attract deer to specific hunting locations at specified times of the hunting season.

This is most readily achieved by planting a variety of cultivars with different growth characteristics, maturation times, and palatability peaks. Some plants do well in dry conditions, others need more moisture, and others do better in the cold. Still others require warm weather. We like to plant a virtual salad bar of highly nutritious cultivars. Multiple cultivar plantings allow us to meet several nutritional needs through a full range of growing conditions. They also provide a "hedge" against single species crop failure.

Peak Plant Palatability

It's important to understand the concept of peak palatability. Peak palatability is that time period when a cultivar is most attractive to deer. It can be as short as a few days and as long as a couple of weeks or more. In our area, palatability changes are most noticeable with brassicas. Deer feed little on spring planted brassicas until the plant experiences a hard freeze or reaches natural maturity. After a good fall freeze, it's as if someone threw the feeding switch. Deer go from a nip here and there to a brassicas "mow-down".

We see a more subtle example during late spring and summer in plots containing a mixture of chicory and clovers. If you get down on your hands and knees and look closely, you'll see how deer repeatedly nip the same variety of clover or chicory. They'll ignore a half dozen or so other clovers and chicories growing an inch or two nearby. This is called peak palatability. Deer key on individual plants at specific times in the cultivar's growth cycle.

This phenomenon is obvious on our "cafeteria test" at the Demo Center. We plant 150 of our 10-x 10-foot test squares with 75 different seeds. Each seed variety is planted in two separate squares. In all, the squares cover a half-acre. The deer can feed cafeteria style in any square they choose. Time after time, we see deer selecting the same two squares in the grid of 150. It's clear they have strong preferences for certain cultivars at specific times. They will feed on a specific cultivar for a week or so then shift to another for what appears to be a specified period of time.

It's important to understand this concept and plant hunting plots according to each plant's peak palatability. Alfalfa is a good example. In our area, most alfalfa plants lose their appeal after a freeze; deer forsake it overnight. It makes little sense to plant a late-season hunting plot in alfalfa. On the other hand, brassicas is very attractive after a hard freeze. That's the cultivar we want in a late-season hunting plot. Conversely, alfalfa can be a great early season draw, especially if the growing season has been droughty and the clovers are struggling.

A handful of (red) cattle clover vs. a handful of deer-forage clover. The differences are obvious. The stemmy lignin-heavy clover on top grows tall and straight for harvest and storage. The clover blend below has fine, delicate stems and would be almost impossible to dry and bale. Different clovers serve different purposes.

Avoid Cattle Forages

When considering food-plot plantings, distinguish between cattle forage and deer forage. Our country has been producing commodity seeds for cattle forage for hundreds of years. As a result, virtually all forage seeds available at seed stores are designed for to feed cattle. The research driving the development of cattle forages sought higher yields of milk or beef. The goal was to create crops that could be harvested and stored in a barn for winter feeding as dry material. That's why so many cattle forages are so stemmy. It's easier to harvest, dry and bale high-standing stemmy forages.

In the late 1980's, however, new blends were developed specifically for deer consumption. The research driving the development of deer forages is designed to produce better venison and antlers, not milk and beef. The forages were developed to be grazed in fields, not harvested and stored inside barns. Many of these cultivars are incorporated into the most popular blends in the industry like the Whitetail Institute.

Clovers are the Key

Clover blends are the workhorse plants for most food plots. Imperial Whitetail clover has been a mainstay of food plot enthusiasts for years and is credited with starting the food plot industry. They can contain about 25 percent or higher protein. Clovers grow during spring, summer and into fall. If you plan to plant a clover plot, you want mixtures of clovers engineered for consumption by white-tailed deer.

Many cattle clovers shoot up quickly in early spring. By June, they're knee-high or taller. We call these "feel-good" clovers, because you feel good when you see them. Unfortunately, they're

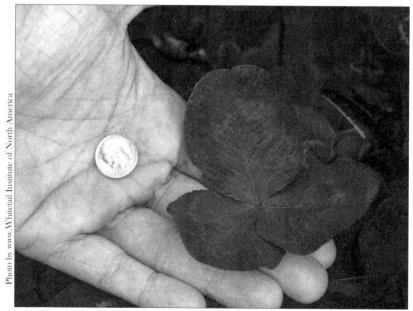

Engineered clovers like this one produce large leaves that are easily digestible by whitetails. A good clover devotes more energy to producing large, digestible leaves than undigestible, tall, thick stems.

not the best for deer. They have a lot of stem material, but not as much succulent, high-protein leafy material. These clovers were developed to be harvested and fed dry to cattle.

Unfortunately, deer don't digest stems well. Stems are high in lignin, which makes stems rigid, and deer digest lignin inefficiently. Cattle, however, digest lignin easily. As a result, most alfalfas and tall stem clovers are best suited to cattle. We like thin-stemmed clovers that grow dense and low to the ground. They're designed for deer consumption in the wild, not for dry feed for barnyard cows. Blended clovers mature at different times and are selectively eaten by picky deer. Low, dense clovers also smother weeds and grasses better than high, stemmy clovers, which is a plus when trying to get multiple years out of food plots. Clovers like these are what you find in name brand food plot blends like those marketed by the Whitetail Institute and other reputable companies.

Clovers should be planted as blends. Almost any clover will do well in spring, but a well-blended clover plot should perform well year-round under all but the most extreme conditions. You achieve this type of performance by using clovers with diverse characteristics, including maturation rate, heat and drought tolerance, cold weather performance characteristics, and, of course, tolerance to grazing. It sounds complicated and frankly it is. Developing seed blends is an art and science best left to the pros. Most high-quality premium forage blends are developed to provide food plot diversity.

Chicory: A Well-Kept Secret

The goal of a hard-working food plot is to cover all weather and growing conditions while providing nutrition and palatability. We're going to put a lot of time, money and energy into the food plot. We don't skimp on seed blends. As a hedge against Mother Nature, we always use clover mixes with chicory, which looks like a dandelion. Chicory is about 25 percent protein, and has a long taproot that's excellent for droughts and hot weather. It's also efficient at transferring minerals from soils to deer. It's also much easier to grow than alfalfa which is very sensitive to soil pH. In a recent drought year at the Demo Center, we went 45 days without rain. Most clover varieties turned brown and dormant. The chicory thrived as if no amount of heat or drought could stress it. Deer stayed on the plots, working the chicory day after day. With a chicory blend, you're pretty well covered through the dry, hot summer periods. We are looking forward to trying a new blend called Chicory Plus™ this spring. As far as we are concerned you can't get enough chicory and clover in a food plot.

Brassicas: Secret Weapon of the North

Northern deer managers need to plant with heavy frost and cold, freezing temperatures in mind. Brassicas plants are rape-like cultivars and are superior cold weather forages. When planted in early spring, brassicas achieves maximum thigh-high growth by fall. When

Brassicas doesn't perform well in low soil pH. Soil pH should be a 5.6 or higher in order for the plant to grow tall enough to supply enough food through the winter. Brassica grows best if planted in soil with a pH between 6.3 and 7.0.

planted in late summer brassicas plants get knee high by the end of the fall growing season. Initially, we only planted brassicas in spring, but recently we have been planting a lot of fall hunting plots in brassicas. In less severe parts of the country brassicas is most often planted in late summer as a hunting attractant and winter food source.

In very good growing conditions, spring planted brassicas can grow waist high; the plant is 34 percent to 38 percent crude protein, and is mostly leaves. Brassicas has a bitter taste when it first comes up, but works well when planted with other forages. Deer use the clover and chicory until brassicas sweetens. If you taste it in mid-summer, it still isn't sweet enough for a salad. After a killing frost, a chemical change occurs, creating sugars. Deer seem to go nuts over brassicas just when our clover and chicory approach dormancy. It's perfect timing. The spring planted waist-high, high-protein brassicas plants provide nutrition and attract deer throughout the hunting season and beyond. With a brassicas planting, you can have tons of forage

Photo by Charles J. Alsehimer

Brassicas becomes highly attractive to Northern deer after a hard frost, snow or freeze. This buck prefers clover and chicory all spring and summer, but is drawn to brassicas during winter.

per acre when deer - especially big bucks - need it most- after the rut. We've found that brassicas plants stay green and upright in cold weather until consumed by deer. This is a real plus in snow country.

Deer paw through the snow and feed heavily on brassicas from November through early March. Our best late-season hunting plots are brassicas-based. Spring green-up occurs in early April in our region. Unfortunately, it's an annual plant and must be replanted each spring. But that's easy. You simply cast new brassicas seed - on top of your plot while the clover and chicory are dormant or just

....

As deer managers, we must be concerned with the herd's overall health. In the North, brassicas is often the only green source of high-protein forage during the late hunting season and beyond.

....

waking up. Brassicas makes its way through the other cultivars to contact the earth and germinate. It will be ready by late summer. Brassicas, when combined with clover and chicory, creates a great three-tiered smorgasbord.

As deer managers, we must be concerned with the herd's over-all health. In the North, brassicas is often the only green source of high-protein forage during the late hunting season and beyond. Alfalfa is already brown and dormant, while standing corn and rye grass are low-protein foods. Brassicas will be used in bow season and gun season, and on through January, February, and into March when all but the browse forages are gone.

By December, mature bucks might lose 25 percent of their body weight because of rutting activity. With a healthy winter supply of brassicas in your food plots, you'll provide deer with a prime food source to regain weight. This ensures you'll retain those bucks for the following season. You don't want to find them piled up in March snow banks. Also, a good winter and early spring diet

Photo by Charles J. Alsehimer

These post-rut bucks are getting a heavy dose of protein just when they need it most. This brassicas plot helps them recover weight they lost during the rut. Next spring, they will convert food into antlers rather than replacing lost weight.

allows a buck to enter the antler-growing season in prime condition and put most of his nutrition into growing massive racks.

In the first 10 years we owned the land now occupied by the research facility, we never saw deer wintering on the highest elevations of our property, which is 2,200 feet. No matter the habitat quality we created, deer always left the high ground for sheltered valleys and south-facing slopes. In those 10 years, we recovered only three shed antlers from more than 500 acres, even though we combed the property each spring. The deer just left the property. It was that simple.

The first year we tried brassicas we checked the property in late January. With 24 inches of snow on the ground, we had to use a snowmobile to reach the plot. To our amazement, we found deer tracks and droppings everywhere. The following spring, we recovered a 2 ½ -year old's shed in the middle of our one-acre test plot. The next summer, we increased the test plot to three acres of brassicas and eagerly waited for winter to see what would happen. The following January, again on a snowmobile, we found the plot littered with tracks and signs of deer pawing through 12 inches of snow to reach the still-green brassicas. When spring arrived, we found three sheds in the field. Now we plant 40% of our food plots with brassicas to nourish deer and give them premium food during winter. No wonder the Whitetail Institute calls their brassicas product "Winter Greens".

One March afternoon, four years after the original planting of our three-acre plot, we found nine sheds lying there. These antlers were from seven different 1 ½-year -old bucks that spent winter on our property. Those guys soon become shooters. In spite of the severe weather at this elevation, deer hang around because the food source is beneficial. If chicory is our summer secret weapon, brassicas is our winter wonder. We can't recommend brassicas enough for cold-weather deer diets. We now find high-quality sheds in almost all of our food plots.

Inoculation: A Shot in the Arm for Seeds

Cultivars such as clovers, alfalfa and beans are called legumes, and they have special, amazing capability. They're able to create their own nitrogen. Legumes draw nitrogen from the air and turn it into a usable nutrient for the plant itself. This process is called nitrogen fixation, and occurs in nodules that form on plant roots when they encounter certain bacteria in the soil.

Scientists have learned that exposing, or inoculating, raw seed to this plant-specific bacteria, increases the germination rate and creates stronger, denser stands of young cultivars. Practitioners, especially weekend food-plot warriors, know that inoculating seed is a royal pain. It's a messy, imperfect process if you don't know what you're doing. For starters, it seems you never can find the right inoculant for the legume you're planting, and when you do locate the right one, you must buy enough to do 100 pounds of seed at a time. Then you must mix it into a slurry and blend it with seed.

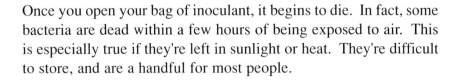

Once you open your bag of inoculant, it begins to die. In fact, some bacteria are dead within a few hours of being exposed to air. This is especially true if they're left in sunlight or heat. They're difficult to store, and are a handful for most people.

What's a fellow to do? Science makes it possible to coat legume seeds with an inoculant and then encapsulate the active seed in a protective layer of hard lime. It's kind of like an M & M candy, where the peanut is the legume seed, the chocolate is the inoculant, and the bright melt-proof sweet coating is the lime.

Almost all high quality food plot forage seeds - at least the legumes-are pre-inoculated by manufacturers. Always look for inoculated seed when buying food plot blends. If you can find inoculated seed that is encapsulated in a protective layer of lime, so much the better. Always check expiration dates, because even encapsulated inoculants lose their effectiveness in a few years.

This mother's milk for seedlings will jump-start your tiny plants and ensure their careers as nitrogen fixers get a good start. Don't waste your money on low-cost seed that has not been inoculated. Without inoculant, seeds don't do well and, frankly, it's too much hassle to inoculate seeds yourself.

Plant Grains to Start a Plot

On areas with marginal soils - i.e., pH in the low 5s - we might not be able to grow premium food plot products until lime kicks in and we raise the pH. In these instances, we like Whitetail institutes "Extreme", which produces a good perennial food plot in poor soil pH. The key to successful "Extreme" planting in poor soil is fertilizer, be sure to fertilize heavy. Annuals, such as wheat and rye also can be used in poor planting conditions. It's a good attractant and can serve as a "place holder" until your soil is ready for high dollar premium blends. If planting annuals, use a blend rather than a straight planting of grain forage.

Corn: OK If You Have The Room

Many people want to plant corn in food plots. We call corn a one-month wonder in areas with a high deer population. Therefore, we don't often plant corn for deer. The young, green corn plant does nothing for lactating does or antler-growing bucks during spring and summer. In fact, if nipped as a young plant, corn will usually fail to grow ears. When it's ready for eating in autumn, it only provides cover and 8 percent protein, at best. In highly populated areas, if corn makes it through the shoot stage, deer will eat the tassel and silk, thus eliminating its ability to grow ears. With corn, your ground is tied up from spring until fall, and all for just a one-and two-week feeding frenzy in August or September. When deer need nutrition most, the ground is brown dirt. It's much better to take that one-acre food plot and try to grow a perennial clover and chicory mix to maximize food benefits for deer.

We want to see edible greens as early in spring as possible. Corn is an excellent energy and high-carbohydrate source, but it's relatively weak in protein. Its principal value comes as a fall attractant, but

Photo by Charles J. Alsehimer

Whitetails love corn, especially in fall and winter. Unfortunately, corn is a "one-month wonder" in most regions, and ties up valuable soils all spring and summer without contributing anything to a deer's nutritional needs. We prefer plots with cultivars that work year-round.

the same is true of some rich, green plots that nourish deer year round. To make matters worse, farmers plant it by the mile, providing stiff competition. Even so, a good, green food plot in corn country provides the variety whitetails crave.

Leave the corn planting up to farmers unless you have acres and acres of food-plot space available for clover and brassicas based forage and corn plantings. If you want to try a corn plot, we recommend do it in large plots and plant a green forage like beans along with it.

Deciding what to plant in food plots can be as easy or difficult as you choose to make it. It is never an exact science and, like all things weather-dependent, Mother Nature has a lot to say about how your plots fare each year.

A little research and planning, however, pays huge dividends. Before selecting a cultivar or cultivar blend, think about the role you've chosen for this planting. Are you creating a quarter-acre green patch for a month of bow season, or do you think you'll provide deer some serious year-round tonnage in a 5-acre plot? Also, do you want the planting to last five years or five weeks?

Analyze seed labels and call seed producers' hotlines with questions. Visit the websites of companies like NorthCountry Whitetails (www.NorthCountryWhitetails.com) and Whitetail Institute of North American (WhitetailInstitute.com). Both companies provide valuable information on selecting cultivars. Be careful with "local seeds" sold at feed-and-seed stores. Chances are, these blends consist of cattle forages.

And finally, don't be afraid to experiment. Try one blend here and another there. Mix and match. Pay attention to the deer and how they respond to your plantings. Above all, have fun. This is not open-heart surgery, nor is it rocket science. If you make a mistake or two, relax, you're in good company. We all make mistakes. Most importantly, don't give up if you suffer a setback with your plantings. There is always next season.

Chapter XIV

Predicting Deer Movement: The Answer is Blow'n in the Wind ⟶

The tram pulls into a large sloped food plot at the foot of a 300-foot ridge. "Must have killed some good bucks here." remarks a guest. "Does yes, mature bucks - no." states Neil, "The big boys hang out 200 yards down the hill where they can scent check the entire 5-acre plot from one thermal wind-funnel. On any given evening hunt,they know everything going on in this plot including who's hunting it. Evening thermals make it impossible to kill a big buck here. They don't use this plot until after we leave. You have to hunt the old deer down in the woods"

Most landowners experience difficulty predicting mature deer movement patterns. Humans approach the woods much differently than deer; they aren't on the same wavelength, they haven't learned how to think like a deer. This is especially true with mature bucks who seem to come and go like ghosts. Understanding deer movement is the key to huting success. You can't harvest deer you can't see.

Preservation of the species dictates that deer must consume food and repro-duce. Deer rely heavily upon their senses to avoid predators. This is espe-cially true during hunting season when they are in constant alert. Of all their senses, their sense of smell has the greatest impact on their movement patterns.

A number of factors contribute to deer movement; the combina-tion of these factors and the maturity of a buck will ultimately determine how that deer will move on any given day. Understanding these factors and how they interact with one anoth-er greatly enhances a hunter's ability to choose the right hunting set up. Understanding deer movement is a complicated process. We have broken it down into a three-step mapping process to make it as simple as possible. We call the process "Mapping Deer Movement" or "MDM" for short.

MDM Step 1: Map Food Sources and Identify Bedding Areas

Day in and day out the most important of these three factors is the consumption of food. The first thing every good land manager must learn is the locations of the highest concentrations of the most attractive food sources on a given property. We call these areas "destination feeding areas" and they represent the baseline for predicting deer movement patterns. These areas change over time as property conditions change.

The Demo Center has many destination feeding areas. These areas will change with the seasons. During the summer and fall months large food plots concentrate high-quality food and become evening destination areas. The plots are a nightly draw as deer travel from bedding areas to consume the high quality forages. As autumn approaches and our oak woods start to drop acorns, deer start to shift from the main destination feeding food plots to areas where the oak trees are producing high-quality mast. That's not to say, that they have abandoned the food plots, they haven't. The buffet table at this time of the year simply included another tasty entrée that happens to be located in our oak woodlands.

When the snow starts to fly and the acorns have been consumed, our deer still focus on the food plots as destination feeding areas but also start to seek out woody browse. Once again, the buffet has changed as

Everything in a deer's world is driven by food. To truly understand your deer, you must fully understand the food sources available on your land.

Neil killed this great 3-1/2 year old buck on the last day of the New York archery season. The buck was killed within 50 yards of a browse cut.

has the location of the table. Heavily timbered areas and browse cuts with lots of regenerating brambles and young trees become destination feeding areas during the late season and winter.

Landowners need to be aware of the food sources on their properties and when these foods become destinations for deer. It helps to actually develop a time line and place each destination feeding area on it to estimate the time of year deer will be drawn to different types of food sources on your property. Once you have a timeline established you should locate these areas on a map of your property.

Aerial photography and satellite images are excellent at providing hunters with a bird's-eye view of their property. A high-quality aerial photograph of your property will prove to be one of the most effective tools when it comes to predicting deer behavior. There are many different types of maps on the market. Some of the best maps combine aerial photographs with topographical lines. These maps can be difficult to obtain but show the greatest amount of detail on a property. Property layout maps need to be big. You also need to be able to identify detail. Select your map based on the resolution and overall size of the map. Good detail costs money but it is more than worth the price when doing layout work. A two-hundred acre piece of property can effectively be displayed on a map 36" x 36". This large map will allow you to pick out details and identify travel corridors that otherwise might be missed.

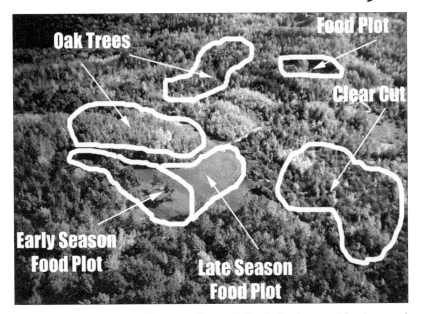

Use a clear transparency film to outline each food plot, browse (clear) cut and mast area. Understanding where the existing destination feeding areas are on a property helps predict deer movements at specific times of the year.

Once you have your map in hand, it's time to draw specific destination feeding areas. Use clear transparency film for your drawings, this will allow you to repeatedly mark-up your map without ruining the original copy. Outline each food plot, browse concentration, and hard and soft mast sources to show concentrations of food.

It is tempting to identify bedding areas as well, but it can be counter productive. Bedding areas can be difficult to identify as they often vary from season to season and day to day. In fact, deer often bed in a variety of areas in a single day. It is therefore, impractical and unnecessary to attempt to map these areas. MDM deals primarily with a mature deer's "final approach" to a known feeding area and exact knowledge of where a given deer beds is not necessary for success.

Now that you know where the deer are headed (food sources), it's time to find out how they're going to get there. Deer approach

the woods in a much different manner than people do. When moving through the woods, deer rely on their sense of smell first and foremost, followed by their sense of hearing and then their eyesight. Humans, on the other hand, rely on their eyesight primarily, followed by the sense of hearing and then the sense of smell. They analyze the woods visually and tend to "stake-out" deer trails or food sources. They typically know enough to hunt down-wind of where they expect deer to be but that's the extent of their "wind thinking."

Mature deer will often remain in thick cover and let their nose do the walking by smelling for danger and other deer.

Deer and humans interpret the woods differently. In order to understand and predict deer movement, you have to think like a mature deer and learn how to "read" the woods as a deer does. To be a good hunter you need to learn how to "smell" the woods.

MDM Step 2: Map the Wind

Over the years we have had the opportunity to analyze deer travel patterns on hundreds of properties and interview thousands of hunters about deer movement. This led to the development of a deer movement model that can generally predict mature deer travel patterns on a given property. Of all the variables affecting mature deer movement in our model we believe wind is the one variable, which best predicts where and how mature deer will move. Time and time again we have found that you can count on a mature buck to "play" the wind to minimize his vulnerability.

Just for a moment envision yourself in the woods during a moderate snowstorm. Everywhere you look snowflakes are riding the air currents, dipping and diving, floating on air. The next time you are actually out in a snowstorm follow individual snowflakes. You will find that in some areas they swirl around while in others they accelerate as they are caught by air currents and are pulled through the woods. In other areas they may float along seemingly without a care in the world. While the movement may seem random, and even chaotic, it is not. Snowflakes go where the wind takes them and the wind is merely reacting to the various forces it encounters in the woods.

We tell our landowner clients to think of a snowstorm as a light switch that, when thrown, can identify the air currents in the woods. The only time the light switches on for humans is when we can see the

This muzzleloader buck was killed by Neil 200 yards down wind of a destination food plot. The buck was killed in a "wind-funnel" used to check for does.

snow riding the air. On the other hand, deer are born into a world where the light switch is on all the time. Their nose can "see" the wind and all it carries. By the time deer reach three or four years of age they understand the wind movement patterns on familiar properties as well as you know your way around your own bedroom. They know how to "see" the woods with their nose. They also know how to minimize vunerability by moving as little as possible. Wind currents and funnels allow deer to check out destination areas long before they arrive.

Wind currents move across terrain in a pattern similar to that of a stream. A constant wind will for the most part follow the path of least resistance; slipping and sidestepping around dense obstacles. Mountains and moderately sized hills will often deflect the air currents enough to change the overall wind direction. A prevailing westerly wind can become a southeastern in the distance of a few hundred feet. Depending on the pattern of hills and dense cover on the property, some areas of increased air velocity will form as the air is deflected and converges into channels and troughs on the property. It's important to stand back and look at the big picture

This wind map of a food plot at the Research Facility shows how the wind concentrates along paths of least resistance. Granted, some wind will penetrate through the trees, most will follow open pathways creating an excellent opportunity for deer to check out the plot from afar.

when it comes to understanding wind. Go for the big picture, as small snapshots of wind direction can be very misleading.

The key to predicting deer movement is to understand wind currents as well as deer do. The easiest way to understand the air currents on a piece of property is to actually map the specific wind currents. In most parts of the country prevailing winds are the norm. That is, winds generally blow out of one, two or at most three directions (covering no more than 180 degrees) most of the time; this is especially true with northern properties. For example, at our research facility the prevailing wind during the early portions of the hunting season is typically south southwest. As early autumn gives way to late fall, around the first of November, the weather pattern starts to switch and we experience more winds out of the north northwest. These prevailing wind patterns are fairly consistent year-to-year and can be used to determine a pattern of prevailing wind based on the time of year.

In the Southern United States, the overall prevailing wind direction is less consistent. Southern winds tend to move in all directions and may not flow consistently enough to map the wind directions. However, the South typically experiences many calm days during hunting season. On calm days, sunlight will create thermals as the air warms and rises while evening temperatures cool the air and cause the air to settle in low spots. Regardless of whether you're mapping prevailing winds or thermals an understanding of how the wind moves will greatly enhance your ability to harvest mature deer.

To map the wind directions for a piece of property, a large working map of the property will be needed, as you will be sketching the observed wind directions on the map in the field. In addition to the map a substance will be needed to allow you to see how the wind moves. Although, milkweed pods and dandelion heads work well; the preferred method for observing wind currents is to use synthetically produced fibers that will float easily on the air. Wind Floaters™ can be purchased at most large hunting supply

During a northwest wind, the air will form "wind funnels" as it flows along terrain breaks in the woods. The scent from the large field can be picked up hundreds of yards away. A mature buck will very likely show up where the arrows converge.

retailers. Smoke bombs work well but they are expensive and harder to find. The final thing needed to map the wind directions on your property is a relatively steady wind. Select a day when the wind is moving at a relatively steady speed of about five to eight miles per hour. Note on the map if it's a sunny day or cloudy day. Direct sunlight will introduce thermal drift into the prevailing wind and alter the overall patterns slightly.

With the maps (topo and aerial photo) in hand choose a base location to establish the actual wind direction. We use our main hunting cabin as our base location. While standing on the deck, we monitor the wind direction with wind floaters and a compass to determine the exact wind direction. Once the overall wind direction has been determined, draw an arrow on the map to represent the wind direction at the base location. The next step is to jump on

During the late summer, milkweed pods mature and burst. Gentle wind currents pick up the "floaters" and drag them along, sometimes for hundreds of yards. Harvested milkweed pods can be used to map wind directions.

the four-wheeler and drive approximately 100 yards. Again, use the wind floaters and compass to determine the wind direction. Draw an arrow on the map to represent the wind direction from specific point where you stopped the four-wheeler.

Once you throw a few wind floaters you'll see that they generally float for about fifty yards before returning to earth. The arrow you draw on the map should roughly represent the distance the wind floater traveled before hitting the ground. Repeat this process over and over across your property. By the end of your mapping exercise you will have hundreds of arrows on your map and a good idea of how the wind moves across your property. Now, during the course of the fall hunting season take time to map the most frequently observed wind directions. Transfer your field mapping to a clear transparency to map each wind direction in order to create a wind map that can be used no matter what the wind direction is during a specific day of hunting. These transparencies will be used in conjunction with your overall property aerial map.

The next step is to interpret the wind patterns you collected. If your land is in hilly and or mountainous terrain you'll undoubtedly notice areas where the terrain has redirected the wind causing it to wrap around the hill or mountain. Depending on how the topography lays out on your property you should notice areas where the wind runs strait and true for hundreds of yards. Yet again, in areas with steep hills you may also notice that the wind in some areas of the property simply swirls round and round and is nearly impossible to map. These "vacuum" areas are typically found on the downwind side of a mountain or hill. The overall wind current is pushed up and over the hill leaving a void on the backside of the hill in which the air falls down and becomes turbulent spinning round and round. These areas of inconsistent wind movement are nearly impossible to hunt and should be avoided during hunting season.

Min-Max Theory of Deer Movement

Once you have mapped the wind directions it's time to understand how deer play the wind. First, young deer are still learning how to play the wind. Expect yearling and two-year-old deer to travel all different directions and not necessarily adhere to any specific movement patterns based on a prevailing wind. This is how they die. Three-year-old bucks who have encountered hunting pressure begin using the wind as a tool to find does and to stay alive. Once the deer has reached four years of age or older it will increasingly rely on the wind to carry maximum information about the world it lives in. They are masters at playing the wind especially when they are moving. They stay alive by minimizing movement and identifying danger long before danger identifies them. We refer to this as the "Min-Max Theory of Deer Movement." Minimize vunerability and movement by maximizing olfactory input (smell).

An analogy that works well is that of a good bird dog. A young pup will work a thick piece of pheasant cover haphazardly charging back and forth covering the ground with his legs not his nose. Sure he already knows how to smell but hasn't figured out how to use the wind to his advantage yet. As the dog spends more time afield and starts to mature it will increasingly favor the downwind side of a cover as it learns that it doesn't need to jump right on a bird, he can smell it from a good distance away. An experienced bird dog will take its time working a piece of cover on the downwind side allowing the wind to carry the scent of birds to his nose. Mature bird dogs have learned that it's a waste of time and much needed energy to charge through every square yard of cover when they can work down wind and allow the air to drift scent of hidden birds to them. The same holds true for mature deer. As a deer becomes older and older they will rely more and more on their nose and minimize movement and the danger associated with it.

Once the deer has reached four years of age or older it will increasingly rely on the wind to carry information about the world it lives in. They are masters at playing the wind especially when they are moving.

"Min-Max" Feeding Strategies

Deer use the wind in different ways at different times of year. Let's follow a mature buck through the fall hunting season. Most states start their hunting season well in the advance of the rut. During the pre-rut mature bucks are focused on two things, consuming food and staying alive. As evening approaches these bucks will typically walk from the bedding area directly into the wind as they make their way to destination feeding areas. If there is any amount of hunting pressure during the pre-rut the deer will move in a defensive posture and use the wind to identify predators directly in their path.

Now let's look at a three acre food plot. Assuming it's a calm evening, about forty minutes before dark the air will start to cool and settle into the low areas of the field. The evening thermals have begun to flow. If the field has any measurable ground slope the heavier cooler air will "roll' downhill through the field. Cool air flows like water in a rainstorm. Envision a field filling with water until it begins to overflow out of the lowest point and then run off through the surrounding woods following the lowest ground points. We refer to these run offs as thermal troughs.

The evening thermals will settle in a similar way, draining the scent out of the field at the lowest point and through the surrounding terrain like a stream. Even terrains create nice wide even air streams; uneven terrains create winding, irregular channels. As a mature deer travels to an evening destination feeding area it will typically walk through the air draining out of the field. By standing in the thermal trough for a few moments (max) it is able determine what deer are already in the field as well as any predators that may be waiting near the field. It will visit these drains before entering a field. He can scent check the entire field from the safety of cover hundreds of yards away.

If you're wondering why you rarely see a mature deer show up on a food plot during daylight hours consider your scent that is draining out of the field and filling his nose a few hundred yards away. No wonder he waits until after dark before entering the field; that's when he gets the "all's clear" from his nose.

"Min-Max" Rutting Strategies

As the fall progresses and the bucks attention starts to turn to breeding he will change his movement patterns as he seeks out receptive does. In a sense, he goes from playing defense to going on the offense. An immature seeking buck will cover lots of ground searching for receptive does. A mature buck has learned that he doesn't necessarily have to walk miles of property to check for receptive does. An immature seeking buck will use the wind as much as possible to deliver information to him about the does in his area; kind of like that old bird dog and the pheasant field.

For a seeking buck to be efficient as he moves about a piece of property, he will typically walk at an angle to the prevailing wind. During the rut it's very common for mature deer to walk at a 45° angle to the prevailing wind. As he walks at an angle to the prevailing wind he is able to gather acres and acres of upwind scent information (max) by traveling only a short distance (min). During the seeking stage mature bucks concentrate on walking in areas where they can obtain the maximum amount of scent by walking shortest distance and incurring the least amount of danger. This is the "Min-Max Theory of Deer Movement" at it 's best.

....

Most properties will have several areas per 100 acres where mature deer can go and let acres and acres of scent information drift past his nose. It's important to identify these "max airflow" areas.

....

Take for example a 50-acre oak wood-lot. Let's assume that it's late morning and ten does and fawns are scattered across the wood lot feeding on acorns. A mature buck will often cruise on the furthest downwind point of the woodlot gathering scent from the deer within the lot. If he's a mature buck he is not only focused on finding does but also identifying predators. By walking a route on the downwind side of the oak flat he'll be able to identify any hunters located within the feeding area. Putting it in financial terms; the mature buck maximizes the return on his investment; and minimizes risk. By contrast, a young buck will often charge right through the center of the oak woods checking out every doe he can find. Sure, he is able to see and smell does but he will miss all the does that are downwind of his line of travel and have to work the woods over and over again. Chances are he will wind up on the receiving end of a broadhead with all of that risky movement.

During the seeking stage mature bucks will often concentrate on finding areas with increased airflow. For example, if your land is located in hilly country two hills merging together will channel the air increasing the amount of area that can be scent checked by a buck passing through. Most properties will have several areas per 100 acres where mature deer can go and let acres and acres of scent information drift past his nose. It's important to identify these "max airflow" areas. During the course of the seeking stage bucks will make frequent stops through these locations as they pass downwind of each individual destination feeding location on the property.

Understanding the fact that mature bucks will generally travel routes where they have the best ability to scent check the greatest area (maximum return on movement) will increase your chances of predicting his movement patterns during the rut. This is when you are most likely to intercept him; this is when he is most vulnerable.

As the breeding season passes mature bucks will again switch gears and focus on consuming food and moving in a defensive posture. During the later stages of the hunting season lessons learned from past hunting pressure will influence a buck's movement patterns as he is now most interested in monitoring potential danger and staying alive.

Late-season bucks are driven primarily by a need to replace the body weight they lost during the course of the rut and avoiding hunters. By moving into the wind they easily can identify predators and avoid hunters. The only chance a hunter has to consistently intercept deer at this time is to allow their scent to travel in a different direction than the deer is traveling. Hunting a destination feeding area will often do the trick but you need to avoid the buck's approach route and stay out of thermal air currents. Bow hunting mature bucks at this time of year can be very tricky.

MDM Step 3: Map Hunting Areas

Mapping destination feeding sites and wind movement will allow you to better analyze the deer dynamics at work on your

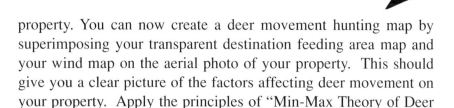

property. You can now create a deer movement hunting map by superimposing your transparent destination feeding area map and your wind map on the aerial photo of your property. This should give you a clear picture of the factors affecting deer movement on your property. Apply the principles of "Min-Max Theory of Deer Movement" in order to identify most likely travel routes and hang outs of the mature bucks using your property.

With map in hand, visit these areas to check for mature buck sign and hunting stand locations. Document which locations will work with specific winds and which won't. Set up your stands and hunt accordingly. We are careful not to overhunt stand locations as mature deer quickly "quit" over-hunted areas. We often find your best chance of killing a mature buck is the first time you sit a given stand. Two sits is about all the pressure a big buck will tolerate before he shifts his travel route to avoid the immediate area of the stand.

Years of observation have taught us that the wind is the key in determining how mature deer move throughout property. To intercept these tough deer you will have to learn how to turn on the lights and see how the air moves across your property. If you can combine knowledge of food sources, how scent moves through and around feeding areas, and apply the "Min-Max Theory of Deer Movement" you are well on your way to harvesting that mature buck you worked so hard to grow.

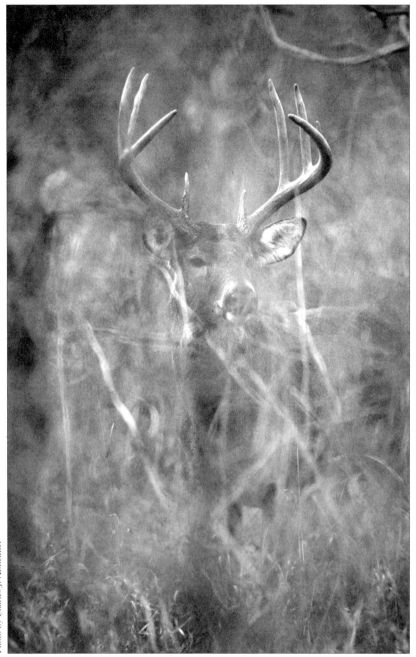

Photo by Charles J. Alsheimer

Chapter XV

Professional Property Layout

The tram pulls into the driveway, the tour complete. Twenty landowners pile off the tram and wave good-by. Two brothers hang back; something's on their mind. We've seen it before, it happens on almost every tour. They've just bought a property and they want to create a whitetail paradise. Could we give them a couple of minutes and take a peek at their map and maybe show them a few things. "Where should we put the food plots? We already have located the sanctuaries. The wind swirls here and here. Could Neil come out and work with them"? It's always the same and always different. Hunters working with their land, land stewards and conservationists in the making. Aldo Leopold would approve.

The key to having a productive and huntable property is to provide everything a deer needs for survival. Most land mangers stop here. We believe in taking it further. In order to have a huntable property, you have to be able to influence deer movement and behavior. Neil's speciality is creating property layouts where deer will consistently bed, move, or feed in a predictable (and huntable) manner.

Can't improve on Mother Nature? Sure you can. A few hours with a chain-saw can dramatically alter the habitat and create areas where deer frequent. The key is in arranging the new landscape in a manner that allows for better hunting.

He uses an in depth understanding of deer behavior and a bag full of habitat manipulation tools. The challenge of property layout is to take what Mother Nature has given you and make it better. Can't improve on Mother Nature? Sure you can. Just work with her; not against her.

Advanced property layout is all about creating and arranging land components like food plots, clear-cuts, sanctuaries and travel corridors. Proper arrangement of the landscape allows you to hunt mature deer successfully. The key landscape factors are topography, wind, security areas and feeding areas. Topography is topography and you work with what you are given. The same generally holds true for wind. Teh rest of the equation is controllable and can be manipulated to your advantage.

Map Your Deer Movement

The first step in the layout process is to map deer movement (MDM). See Chapter XIV for details.

To create a MDM, use arial photos, topos and a clear transparency to analyze how your property components together to influence deer movement. Critical to the analysis is understanding the "Min-Max Theory of Deer Movement" which is also presented in Chapter XIV. The purpose of this mapping is to identify naturally occurring travel routes and hunting areas.

Good naturally occurring stand sites are places where deer are forced to move with a cross wind instead of their preferred head wind. Mark them on your map. In addition to locating areas where deer are vulnerable, search out areas where deer have the ability to bed and move directly into the wind as they approach destination feeding areas. Deer moving directly into the wind are seldom vunerable to hunting (especially bowhunting) as their sense of smell enables them to identify a hunter's presence from hundreds of yards away. Mark these as well. Some of these areas can be made condusive to hunting by manipulating the habitat if possible. Red zones; don't hunt or manipulate. Green zones; hunt.

Neil has laid out hundreds of properties and has concluded that on most properties Mother Nature favors deer over hunters. For instance, many tree and brush species seed themselves with the help of the wind. Unfortunately, (for the hunter) wind distributed seed creates cover bands which generally lie along the path of prevailing wind currents. The end result is a series of nearly impossible to hunt travel corridors of cover. Perfect for the deer; hell for the hunter. If your deer are generally moving in the wrong direction and are always difficult to hunt, you need to change their movement patterns. This is what advanced property layout is all about.

Manipulate Deer Movement

To manipulate the deer movement patterns, you will need to create areas of safe haven (sanctuaries) or thick cover to channel deer movement. Early on during our management program at the research facility we carved out a 3 ½-acre destination food plot located about 100 yards directly downwind of thick bedding cover. Unfortunately, due to the large field size and the naturally occurring deer movement patterns, we found that it was nearly impossible to intercept large bucks as they traveled to the destination feeding area. To correct this problem we reprogrammed our deer movement patterns. A new sanctuary was located approximately 200 yards away from the existing field. The 10-acre safe haven was heavily cut to promote regeneration and the super dense holding cover that subsequently followed. The location of this sanctuary was designed to force deer to travel across the prevailing wind as they journeyed to the food plot.

But, it took more than creating a new sanctuary to change behavior. The deer were reluctant to change bedding areas. To correct this, we spent a couple of summers walking through the original bedding location. Within a year or two we had put enough scent and human pressure on the original bedding location so as to "encourage" the deer to bed in the newly created "off limits" sanc-

Creating a new bedding sanctuary can be relatively easy, the basic premise is to make the area as thick as possible. A large dozer can run over and crush young trees to the ground creating immediate bedding cover. Deer started to bed within the crushed tree area within thirty days.

tuary. This is just one example of how deer can be reprogrammed to move in a manner that benefits hunters.

Attracting Deer: Food, Cover and Security

There are three main tools that can be used to attract deer to a specific area. The easiest way to attract deer is with food, increasing native food production and food plots work best. In addition to using food to attract deer, cover is also effective. Thick, six foot and under cover will also influence deer movement. The final way to attract deer to a specific location is to just stay out of that area. Sanctuaries are one of the simplest tools available to land managers for manipulating deer movement. It's a safe bet, if you don't walk into a 15-acre area, deer will concentrate themselves there.

Making an area more attractive to deer will not necessarily change their travel patterns. It depends upon the wind and terrain. Human pressure can be used to your advantage by spending time in areas where you would rather deer didn't frequent. Taking the dog for a walk in the woods on a regular basis is a surefire way to direct deer movement patterns away from a specific area. In addition to using human pressure you can allow the woods to mature into people habitat in areas where you would rather deer didn't travel. But, this takes time. Remember, deer are eating machines. If they are on their feet they are trying to browse, if you allow the forest canopy to close in some areas it will dramatically decrease the amount of available browse per acre and steer deer away from a location.

A Case Study

To layout a piece of property, use all of the habitat management tools at hand to try and create predictable travel patterns. For example, a 200 acre piece of property was recently purchased by one of Neil's consulting clients. Overall, the property was heavily forested with no food plots and very little agriculture surrounding

This property was recently purchased by one of Neil's clients. The land is dominated by woods with very little space available for food plots. Notice the fields surrounding the property, as it stands right now deer will have to leave the property to feed.

the property. The landowner wanted to consistently harvest three year old or older bucks.

Neil's initial site evaluation of the property indicated that the property suffered from a serious lack of high-quality foods during the critical antler developmental months. Very little agriculture was found in the area so food plots would play a critical role in the overall property management scheme. In order to achieve the landowner's goals of heavy antlered three-year-old bucks, a goal was set to clear 10% of the overall property and replant with high-quality food plots.

The property had been purchased from a logging company and had recently been logged. The open tree canopy created by the removal of mature trees would soon start to regenerate new trees and briars on the property. The volume of food per acre within the woodlots would triple within the next few years. The heavy cutting will greatly enhance the ability of the property to hold and feed mature whitetails. The logging operation also left a network of skidder roads throughout the property.

Locating Food Plots

First, we needed to locate sites for high quality food plots. The most obvious choice for a destination feeding food plot on this property is a brushed over power line (A). The old power line will be relatively easy to clear and prepare for planting. This site will work very well because the majority of the cover located on the property is located up wind of the destination feeding area. Whenever possible locate

Destination Food Plots A and B are located on the down wind side of the property. This will allow for easier hunter access.

destination-feeding areas on the furthest downwind side of your property (stay away from neighbors). Location A limits wooded cover downwind of the field and increases hunters chances of ambushing deer as they travel to the field.

Although the power line was quite large, more food plots will be needed to reach the 10% planting goal. The next step was to site a secondary destination feeding field within the woods. This plot location was selected based on the overall topography of the area and soil quality. A relatively dense stand of pines was chosen as the location for the second plot B. A heavy-duty bulldozer would be required to clear the ground in advance of planting. This plot was near the center of the property but wind direction would allow easy

When an isolated destination feeding field (B) is located in the woods, mature deer often just hang around directly down wind of the field and monitor other deer and predators that may be in the field. With this scenario, it's nearly impossible for hunters to hunt the field or sneak into the "monitor" location without alerting the deer.

hunter access. Whenever possible, locate destination feeding fields well within the parameters of your property, this will allow for deer using the plot to spend more time within the boundaries of your property and remain safe from neighbors.

When a large, isolated destination-feeding plot is located in the woods it's necessary to create satellite hunting food plots. Without satellite hunting food plots an isolated field is too easy for mature bucks to monitor. A mature deer will simply bed 200 yards downwind of the field in a scent funnel and allow the field scent to drift to his nose. In laying out property you must always be mindful of the "MDM Theory of Deer Movement"(see Chapter XIV). Rutting bucks are hunting your property in a similar manner as you. They know where the does are heading each night. A mature buck would prefer to simply camp out downwind in a scent trough and check out the field from a distance. Concentrating deer in one isolated area and a mature buck will not have to move far to check for does. This limits his vunerability (movement). If you want to have any hope of harvesting a mature buck you need to force him to keep moving in order to check does on food plots.

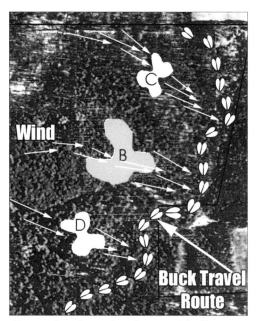

The trick to create a productive hunting layout is to spread out several food sources within the immediate area. Satellite hunting food plots C and D are both located within 200 yards of the primary destination feeding plot. Now, if a smart old buck wants to use his nose he

By spacing three plots in a straight line perpendicular to the prevailing wind will force deer using their nose to investigate the plot to walk six hundred yards and allow a hunter a chance to intercept.

will have to walk between three food plots in order to smell all the does in the area. Using several small plots in a linear pattern over the span of 500 yards will force deer to move and offer a much greater chance of harvest than if the plots are isolated by themselves. In this case the buck will have to walk over 600 yards to smell for does, easily creating an opportunity for a hunter to sneak into his path.

More food plots are needed in order to reach our feeding goal of 10%. Two additional satellite hunting food plots were located on the property. Location F is an outstanding hunting location. With the prevailing Northwest wind location F is the furthest downwind portion of the property. This location is an ideal staging place for deer that are trying to monitor the property with their noses. To increase the concentration of deer in this staging area create a Boomerang-shaped hunting food plot. (See Chapter X). Late in the season brassica plants are sure to attract even the most elusive whitetails to this location. Don't worry about the close proximity to the destination food plot A, plot F is only made better by the large field A. Deer using plot A will naturally swing into plot F as

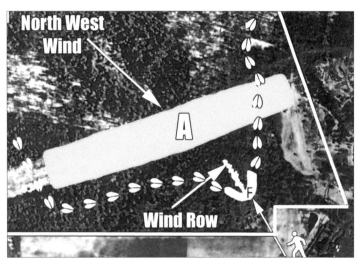

Food Plot F should be the most consistent place to harvest mature deer. Note the easy hunter access and tendency for mature bucks to checking out A to pass through F.

they check for does and danger in the big field. Not only is this plot a great location to intercept a big deer it's also easy to hunt. Hunters simply can walk around the woods in the open grassy field and then travel a short distance in the woods to the plot. Keeping hunters out of the woods helps reduce the pressure and will make it difficult for deer to pattern hunter movement.

An additional hunting food plot was located within an old abandoned log landing. Site G is on the down wind of the property and easily can be cleared with just a few hours with a bulldozer and a skilled operator. Sometimes the best hunting food plots take advantage of already existing openings.

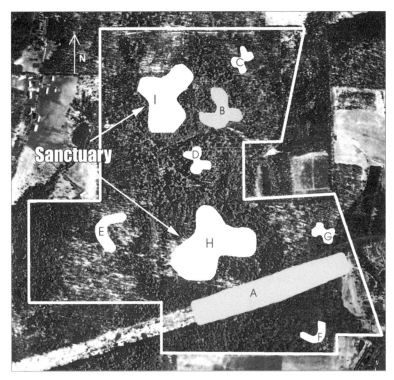

Once food plot locations are established, it's time to add sanctuaries up wind of food sources. This arrangement favors hunting. Two primary sanctuaries will concentrate deer upwind of Destination Food Plots A and B.

The vast majority of food plots located on the property are on the eastern side of the land. In order to balance this out, one more final hunting food plot was located in area E. Area E uses the neighbor's field located just north and west as a barrier. Deer moving through the area will be traveling approximately 80 yards east or downwind of a large open field. Food Plot E is located right in

Increasing the quantities of native plant growth is always a very important part of a good land management plan. Selective timber harvest and clear cuts open the forest canopy and produce tons of food and cover.

the middle of the naturally occurring travel corridor. The trees and brush cleared from food Plot E will be piled directly downwind of the plot forcing deer to travel through the plot as they pass through the area. Plot E also can be hunted when the wind changes direction and blows from directions other than northwest.

Seven food plots in various sizes and shapes have been located across the property. With the exception of the power line field, a bulldozer will be used to clear each of the food plots. The overall acreage of the land cleared totals 15 acres. This number still falls below the 10% goal for planting. Logging roads located within the property will be planted with a blend of clover and chicory to easily make up the remaining five acres needed to reach the antler enhancing 10% planting goal.

Locating Sanctuaries

Once the food plots are located it's time to use sanctuaries for holding deer. For this program 20% of the property was earmarked for sanctuaries. Two main sanctuaries were located. Sanctuaries I and H were located in close proximity to the food plots. The sanctuaries will create a safe haven and concentrate deer up wind of destination feeding areas. Within a year mature bucks will be using the sanctuaries.

Deer move from sanctuary to sanctuary and from sanctuary to food sources. They enable you predict deer movement and accurately position hunting locations.

Maximize Native Plant Growth

Increasing the quantities of native plant growth is always a very important part of a good land management plan. Selective timber harvest and clear cuts open the forest canopy and produce tons of food and cover. In order to promote more native plant growth seven acres of clear cuts were scheduled for cutting. Rather than locate one large cut, smaller "browse cuts" will be used to create areas of regeneration. All trees except for mast producing trees were selected for harvest within the browse cuts. Within two years the cut over areas will have provided pockets of escape cover. In addition to creating great cover, browse cuts also offer high-quality browse. Again, because the browse cuts will concentrate food and cover, they should be located in a linear pattern preferably crosswind to prevailing wind currents. The idea is to have a buck cruise from one area of cover to the next as he searches for does.

The travel corridor will keep deer travel within the thick corridor and allow the deer to drift downwind to each individual food plot.

Add Travel Corridors

The final touch for this particular management plan will be the layout of travel corridors. Ideally, you would like to have your

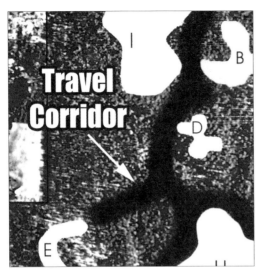

Cutting timber in 50-yard wide bands will concentrate cover and create deer highways.

bucks cruising along the upwind side of linear food plots C, B and D. If this happens they're more likely to swing downwind and into the food plots offering a shot, then return back to the previous line of travel. Deer often travel through freshly cut tree tops as they offer excellent cover. To create a travel corridor, trees will need to be cut in order to increase cover (tops and regeneration) within the travel corridor. Cutting trees during the late summer months or during the winter will create different types of cover in travel corridors. Summer tree cutting creates more immediate cover for deer; leaves often remain on cut trees well into the hunting season, offering food and cover. Winter cutting will promote more natural regeneration of stump shoots. In the case of this property cover is needed immediately therefore trees will be cut during the summer months and be allowed to fall in place. The travel corridor will keep deer travel within the thick corridor and allow the deer to drift downwind to each individual food plot.

Plant Strategically

To fine-tune the management plan food plots will be planted with different types of forages to draw deer to specific areas during different times of the year. The two destination feeding fields will be planted in a blend of clover and chicory. These food sources will consistently remain attractive to deer throughout the entire growing season. Whitetail Institutes Chicory Plus will provide

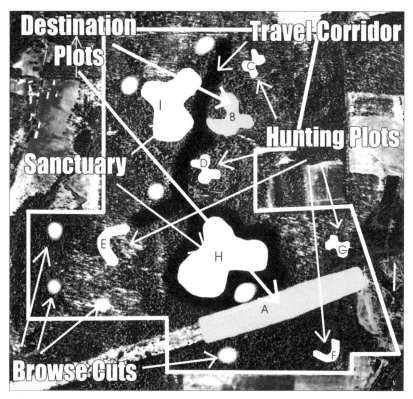

This layout goes far beyond the basics of providing food and security. The manipulation of the elements in this layout creates dozens of huntable areas and will allow hunters to harvest mature deer. Most properties are in need of additional elements. Elements should always be added with an eye toward creating a huntable property. Close attention to detail prior to performing the work is worth the effort.

high quality forage during the critical antler development and fawn raising stages. The satellite hunting food plots will be planted with hunting mixes that will focus deer to particular plots during the fall hunting season. For example, food plot F can easily be hunted during a northwest wind. In this part of the country a cold and blustery northwest wind can be expected during a later portion of the hunting season. This location should not be planted with an early season food source that stops growing or dies in cold weather, instead, use a food that matures with the cold weather. Brassica planted in plot F will become more attractive to deer as the weather turns frosty and cold. In this case, Whitetail Institute's Winter

Greens will be used. Matching the plants, plot and wind direction ensures that deer will visit the plot when you want them there.

Neil's client's property is well on its way to becoming an excellent hunting property. A thorough understanding of deer behavior coupled with a bag full of habitat tricks converted a so-so property to one with enormous hunting potential. Years of hunting enjoyment are sure to follow.

....

Professional property layout is more than adding a couple of food pltos and creating a few secure areas..... Many wildlife consultants don't hunt.. Others hunt but have not mastered the art of property layout for hunting mature deer.

....

Don't stop with the basics. The above case study shows the advantages of a well-thought out hunting property layout. Professional property layout is more than adding a couple of food plots and creating a few secure areas. Professional property layout will enable you to harvest the mature whitetails you have worked so hard to grow. There's a huge difference between harvesting immature bucks and old-timers who know how to take care of themselves. When seeking professional help, be sure to check out the "professionals" credentials in the hunting department. Many wildlife consultants don't hunt. Others hunt but have not mastered the art of property layout for hunting mature deer.

A properly laid out property not only provides whitetails with the habitat diversity they need to thrive but also increases your chances of harvesting mature deer. Time spent with proper property layout is time well spent. Property layout can also get tricky and the work you do on your property will be semi-permanent. Money spent on professional assistance is money well spent. Don't be afraid to seek help when you need it.

A professional layout should include a map identifying where the various habitat elements should be located. It should also identify prime hunting areas based upon MDM. The easy part is growing food plots, planting trees and cutting timber. The tough stuff is creating a property that holds mature bucks and maximizes hunting success.

Chapter XVI

Quality Deer Hunting

Your NorthCountry tram tour of the Demo Center is complete, but you have one more stop. You open the screen door and enter the Demo Center headquarters. Evidence of the hunt surrounds you. Every set of antlers taken in previous years adorns the walls. There must be 50 sets or more. Placed in order by year taken, the antlers show you the project's progress and success. Spikes, forks, and small 6-pointers represent the first two years. Antlers that score in the 100-class occupy the slots for years three, four and five. Then, the record-book bucks start and continue. An occasional fork horn or small 6-pointer bears witness to a young hunter's first deer or an old timer's last. Shed antlers hanging on a post tell the same story, from spikes to record-book class bucks. Photos preserve the smiling faces of successful hunters. It's clear that camp "Kindred Spirits" practices Quality Deer Hunting.

Quality Deer Hunting (QDH) is our version of Quality Deer Management (QDM). By calling it Quality Deer Hunting, we put the

This cabin is the center of hunting activity on the Demo Center. Dubbed "Kindred Spirits," its name portrays the camp's fellowship and sense of family. It's a one-for-all and all-for-one camp, where Quality Deer Hunting is practiced without many hard-core rules and regulations.

emphasis on creating a quality hunting experience, which includes seeing and hunting mature deer. We're not convinced we can actually manage a deer herd, because of the size of our property, but we know we can manage the quality of our deer hunting experience.

At camp Kindred Spirits, we embrace; no, we worship the notion of Quality Deer Hunting. We hope this book helps you create a quality deer hunting experience, and helps you to develop a deer hunting philosophy that maximizes your deer hunting enjoyment.

In our view, nothing beats seeing wild deer benefiting from the habitat-improvement projects you undertake and complete over years. Nothing beats going to bed at night, muscles aching, knowing that today you were a good steward of the land. This book has shown you how to create habitat and be a good steward of the land. But that's only part of the equation. The other part is enjoying quality deer hunting; the ultimate pay off.

Follow QDM Guidelines

We embrace the principles of QDM as outlined by the Quality Deer Management Association. We aggressively harvest does, let young bucks mature, and create favorable habitat and food to sustain a healthy herd. We're active members of the QDMA (Craig is currently Chairman of the National Board of Directors) and have benefited greatly by attending their meetings and reading their magazine, Quality Whitetails. But because of the limited size of our property,

In our view, nothing beats seeing wild deer benefiting from the habitat-improvement projects you undertake and complete over years. Nothing beats going to bed at night, muscles aching, knowing that today you were a good steward of the land.

500 acres, and a few cooperating neighbors, another 1,000 acres or so, we don't believe we're actually managing the deer herd in the true sense of controlling population, sex ratio age structure etc. Thus, we avoid using the term management. We are managing our property and our hunting experience, which is key, but we really aren't managing deer herd dynamics in the truest sense of the word.

Harvest Does Heavily

The fundamental principles of QDM include harvesting does to create a better doe-to-buck ratio and keep the population in check. We aggressively harvest does. In our area and probably in yours, the ratio should be two or less does per buck. There is only so much carrying capacity on any property. If our resident population is 90 percent does, it decreases our chances to harvest bucks in general. There will be fewer to hunt; the math is simple.

Another reason to harvest does has to do with reproduction. When fewer does are available to breed, more mature bucks do most of the breeding season in a shorter time. In areas with far too many does per buck, and too many deer in general, the breeding season can last three months or more, because not all does are bred the first time they enter estrus. This forces the 3 ½-to 5 ½ -year-old bucks to run for 90 days or more as does keep coming into estrus every 28 days until they conceive. During this time, bucks take on little food, and lose body weight just before the onset of winter. This routine runs them into the ground, stresses breeding bucks enormously, and causes more of them to succumb to winter's ravages. Furthermore, does bred during the later breeding seasons drop fawns later in summer. This leads to smaller fawns as autumn and winter approach, which leads to a higher winter mortality rate on fawns.

We try to keep the deer population in check by aggressively harvesting does. We take all the does that New York State will allow us to legally harvest, as long as we believe the ratio is no less than two or three does per buck. If we ever reach a more favorable ratio, we would probably back off on doe harvests for perhaps one season. We use all the meat we can eat, and often contribute to New York's Venison Donation Coalition Program. Each year, dozens of hungry families enjoy high protein, chemical and steroid free venison taken from our property. One deer provides about 160 servings of meat. We encourage hunters every-where to share their har-

These boxes of donated venison create thousands of high protein meals. Hunters feeding the hungry with donated venison is a great idea and a boon to deer managers who need to harvest does.

vest with the needy through one of the excellent venison-donation programs in their area. With deer numbers on the rise and hungry people
in every community, it's a win-win situation. This is one sure fire way
to increase the quality of your hunting experience.

One note of caution. We believe you can harvest does too heavily. For many years deer biologist preached the gospel of harvesting does. The popular wisdom became-you couldn't kill enough.
We probably agree with this adage in the South but would urge you
to use caution in the North. It is harder to recruit new deer into the
herd in the North especially in areas of marginal whitetail habitat
(which is becoming just about everywhere thanks to the destruction
of habitat by deer).

In the last five years we "put on the doe killing breaks" during
two separate seasons. We just weren't seeing the animals and were
reluctant to take the population down below a certain critical mass.
Yes, they come and go from our property but the neighbors were
seeing even fewer does and fawns.

We have also heard some very convincing stories from some
very reliable sources about deer being "shot out" from certain areas.
"Shot out"? Probably not. Scarce, and well below hunter satisfaction level? You bet.

We confess, we like seeing deer in the woods. We probably
could have taken a few more does those years but it seemed like the
right thing to do. One thing for certain we were in a better position
to make this decision than a biologist staring at a computer model
500 miles from our property. Use common sense and don't kill
them all just because the state says you can; enough said.

Let Young Bucks Walk

One of our goals has always been to create a more mature buck
age structure within the herd by allowing young deer to grow up.

Harvesting bucks that are at least 2 ½ -years-old ensures you'll have 2, 3 and occasionally 4 and 5-year-old bucks on the property. To identify a 2 ½ -year-old buck, look for an antler spread as wide as the deer's ears; this works in most parts of the country. The key is to learn to age bucks on the hoof. Generally, this is done by evaluating a combination of antler mass, spread and overall deer size.

We don't get so hung up on harvest rules and regulations that it interferes with our hunting enjoyment. If a hunter mistakes a button buck for a doe, there is no chastisement, penalty or disgrace.

Our 2 ½ -year-old bucks weigh between 160 and 180 pounds on the hoof, but that's a regional index. The visual difference between a 1 ½ -and a 2 ½ -year-old buck is obvious.

Once you start seeing 2 ½ -year-olds and above, you'll recognize differences in body sizes more easily. The more deer you see and compare notes on, the better. Video cameras and motion-triggered cameras will help you age deer in your area.

Counting points can be deceptive. With proper nutrition, 1 ½ -year-old bucks often sport 8-point racks or better. We've seen 1 ½ -year-old 10-pointers show up on the meat pole. Like all things, you get better at aging animals with practice. Pay attention and practice, and soon you'll be batting almost 100 percent, at least on bucks age 2 ½ and older.

We do not, however, get so hung up on harvest rules and regulations that it interferes with our hunting enjoyment. If a hunter mistakes a button buck for a doe, we don't chastise, penalize or disgrace. Even experienced hunters make mistakes.

Bill Walters, a sheriff and friend from Pennsylvania, and one of our camp regulars, once mistook a button buck for a 1 ½ -year-old

These two bucks are a couple of years apart. The buck on the left looks nice, but is far from being his companion's equal. Note the differences in body size and antler development. The more you study deer in the wild, the better you become at aging deer on the hoof.

doe. His arrow found its mark, but 30 minutes later he was back at camp, head hung low, his apology well-rehearsed. We couldn't help but laugh at his unnecessary remorse. We told Bill this is not open heart surgery. We're here to hunt and have a good time. Of course, we teased him, but it was good natured and only added enjoyment to our hunt. Some clubs and managers overdo the rules. We don't punish honest mistakes, and we don't force anyone to hunt big bucks exclusively.

Young Hunters Get the Green Light

We also encourage young hunters and, for that matter, hunters in their later years, to shoot any deer they choose, including yearling bucks. Research shows young hunters who don't experience success drop out of hunting at an alarming rate. We believe young hunters should harvest a few deer as soon as possible after they start hunting. If those deer are yearling bucks, so be it. We want youngsters to embrace hunting whole-heartedly. We will always have yearling bucks to pass up.

The same is true for newcomers. Hunters in their teens and early 20s, and even some in their 30s, get the green light to kill young bucks and - of course - does when hunting with us. That is part of our Quality Deer Hunting formula.

We rejoice and celebrate our fellow hunter's success and are not too tough on their failures. We're truly a one-for-all and all-for-one group. In fact, we dubbed our cabin "Kindred Spirits" on the day we broke ground for it. Our only rule is "no yelling at anyone for any reason". This is a rule taken from Rick Bass' terrific book, The Deer Pasture. That's probably the most important rule anyone could have in a deer camp.

....

Our goal is to harvest mature bucks that are in the top 10 percent age structure of deer on our property. This sets a reachable standard of accomplishment, and keeps those of us who live in the world of marginal soils from judging ourselves against Iowa, Illinois or Kansas standards.

....

Follow the 10 Percent Rule

We also try not to get hung up with antler inches. When setting the bar, we use a 10 percent rule. We talk about antler size in inches so we have a common vocabulary, but our goal is to harvest mature bucks that are in the top 10 percent age structure of deer using our property. We advise you to do the same. It sets a reachable standard, and keeps those of us who live in the real world of marginal soils from judging ourselves against standards set for Iowa, Illinois or Kansas.

Location does not affect the 10 percent rule, nor does the maturity of the deer and your management program. Some areas of the country grow bigger deer because it's easier for them to grow old. Or maybe deer in that area benefit from exceptional nutrition. At our place, a top 10 percent buck will be a 4 ½ -year-old, 140-class buck. That same 4 ½ -year-old buck in Iowa could be 180 to 190 inches. By thinking in terms of the top percent, you can have a trophy challenge no matter where your property is located and how far you're into our program. You should always be proud of harvesting a top 10 percent buck, even if he nets no more than 90 or 100 points in antler score. We like this sliding scale with its ever-present realistic challenge.

Every year we seem to raise the bar a little higher. Three years into our program, we were thrilled to harvest a 2 ½ -year-old deer. After 15 years in our program, we raised the bar to 3 ½ - and 4 ½ -year-old bucks. Some day, the top 10 percent bucks on our place

This 150-plus B&C buck was taken by Craig the last day of the 2002 gun season. In doing so, he raised the 10 percent bar a bit higher for the seasons that followed. We went from forks and spikes to this in about six years. That's truly amazing!

might be 5 ½ -year-olds. We have seen bucks on our land with more than 150 inches of antlers. In fact, Craig shot one this size in 2002. Every buck we kill goes on the wall.

Our sanctuary concept helps our deer reach maturity. Our high-quality food plots increased their weight and antler mass. Our records show a weight increase of 15 percent in the same age and sex categories, when compared to five years before, rack sizes increased dramatically. We like to think this is because of our quality habitat and hunting program.

During bow season the first year we owned the property, we saw seven bucks, including one "rack" buck, a 2 ½ -year-old. We shot no deer that year with a bow. During the firearms season, we shot one 3-point buck. We rejoiced over our first buck kill. We had seven hunters. We did not hunt does.

After four years of habitat-development work, we were passing up yearling bucks, and our "shooters" were 2 ½-year-olds, 100 class bucks and above. We had increased the percentage of 2 ½ -year-old bucks to 25 percent of all antlered deer sighted. After 12 years in our program, we expected to see three bucks per hunter per sit, and it's not uncommon to have four hunters see 15 different bucks, half of which are 2 ½ -year-olds. In 2002, 65 percent of the 68 different bucks we sighted were 2 ½ years old or better.

Our "shooter bucks" became 3 ½ -year-olds with 125 Pope & Young inches and above. Those are dramatic results, especially for western New York State. Sure, these bucks stray off the property and get shot by neighbors, but interestingly, now that the neighbors know they're likely to see one of "our" bigger deer, they're waiting longer and passing more smaller bucks than ever before. They often wind up "settling" for a doe or two for the freezer. They inadvertently are following the harvest principles of QDM. Happily, some got hooked, joined the QDM, and now read the magazine and participate in the organization.

Neil took these two buck on back-to-back evening hunts. The 120 B&C bow buck, shot on the last day of archery season, was followed by the 130 B&C gun buck taken the first day of gun season. Talk about quality hunting.

Even so, we know others are just out there waiting for one of the Dougherty's big ones. We don't get worked up about it. We're just happy more young bucks are growing up in our area. When a neighbor kills one of "our" big bucks, that brings him one step closer to becoming a QDM disciple. Remember one thing when your neighbor kills that trophy you fed and watched all summer, another will soon be there to take his place.

Quality hunting is about lots of things. It's about sitting on a food plot you created, and seeing does and fawns enjoying 35 percent protein forages. It's about watching young bucks sparring and chasing does, and seeing full-racked yearlings instead of spindly spikes. It's about a well defined rut with crapes and rubs, and chasing, snorting and grunting. It's about kinship and friendship, and perhaps most of all, it's about stewardship. Quality hunting adds a special satisfaction that hunting alone cannot deliver.

But the real rush comes from knowing that a top 10 percent deer is out there, and could step out at any moment. You see his rubs on 6-inch trees and his tracks in the soft earth, every shift is a duel. You function at heightened awareness, because you know he's out there. He's the one you're after, the one you read about and saw on TV.

This excitement, combined with the camaraderie of friends and family, is how we define Quality Deer Hunting. We encourage you to create your own quality hunting experiences. This kind of hunting requires time, commitment, planning and some investment, but it's more than worth it.

Join the Quality Deer Management Association

We also suggest you join the QDMA so you can enjoy its many benefits. Attend the group's meetings and read its magazine, Quality Whitetails. You will be encouraged by the success stories of QDMA members, and meet people with management goals similar to your own. It's kind of a support group for people like us.

We state unequivocally that you'll succeed if you follow the principles and practices outlined in this book. You will create better habitat and, ultimately, will have quality deer and Quality Deer Hunting.

We have one final suggestion. Take the following reality check:

Answer "Yes" or "No" to these questions with brutal honesty. If you answer "No" to even one question, it is best to rethink whether you are ready to undertake Quality Hunting and Habitat Development Programs. Try to change each "No" to a "Yes" before going further.

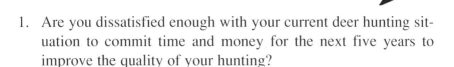

1. Are you dissatisfied enough with your current deer hunting situation to commit time and money for the next five years to improve the quality of your hunting?

2. Are your hunting partners and family of a like mind, and willing to make similar commitments?

3. Do you now, or will you soon, have enough control over a hunting property through a lease or ownership to control how it is hunted, and will you be able to implement habitat-improvement projects on the property?

4. Do you have enough time, money and/or other assets like farm or logging equipment to support a sustained (minimum of five years) commitment to improving the quality of deer hunting on your property?

5. Do you believe, after reading this book and gathering other informative articles, that you have enough knowledge and resources to undertake a program on your own? Or are you prepared to hire a professional to assist with your management plan, and do you know how to contact one?

6. Are you a member of Quality Deer Managemen Associationt?

If you answered "No" to any of the questions, you must analyze why you answered "No," and assess the likelihood of turning each negative answer into a "Yes." In our experience, one or more "No's" will lead to frustration and failure.

If you have honestly answered "Yes" to all five main questions, you are probably ready to go and will improve the quality of deer hunting on your property.

Afterward

Aldo Leopold has had a major influence on the Quality Deer Management Association's philosophy and on that of its founder Joe Hamilton. Leopold has also had a profound effect on Craig's thinking, writing and wildlife managment philosphy. Craig's essays "Something's Happening Here", "Steering True North", and "Creating Leopold Landscapes: An Idea Revisited" led "Quality Whitetails" Editor Lindsay Thomas to establish a permanent magazine department. The department appears in each issue of the "Quality Whitetails" and is designed to showcase QDMA member's properties and reinforce the message of good land stewardship. "Creating Leopold Landscapes: an Idea Revisited" was written for and appear in the QDMA's 2006 food plot book "Quality Food Plots". The following essays ("Steering True North" and "Somethings' Happening Here") are included to bring perspective to "Grow 'Em Right."

"Steering True North"
an Essay by Craig Dougherty

Everyone needs a compass; especially when setting out on a new journey over untraveled territory. Aldo Leopold is our compass. He points "True North". His writings have kept my son Neil and I on track as we converted our 500-acre Steuben County hunting property from an uninteresting expanse of woods with mediocre wildlife habitat and deer hunting to a patchwork quilt of food plots, woodlots, brushy cover, wooded expanses and wet areas.

Today, our land has excellent deer hunting, and a healthy population of ruffed grouse, woodcock, rabbits and squirrels. It is home to dozens of songbirds and birds of prey as well. It is a stopover place to migrants and our ponds and marshy spots hold an assortment of waterfowl. A host of small game and wild critters keep our four legged predators well fed. The occasional bear passes through leaving fresh tracks in the mud. The abundance of wildlife using our property today is a direct result of the habitat we created and a never-ending source of joy to us. We have created a virtual "Leopold Landscape".

Like so many other landowner-hunters today, we focus most of our energy on the white-tailed deer. We practice Quality Deer Management on our property and for the past 15 years and have worked tirelessly to improve the quality of our deer and our deer hunting. We have had more than our share of hunting success and would be lying if we said that our success wasn't in part, measured by an official Pope and Young tape measure stretched across sets of antlers taken from mature white-tailed bucks. It is, and we make no apologies for it. We love hunting big whitetails as much as the next guy and ostensibly is why we purchased the property.

But with time, we began to find ourselves noticing other signs of success. Softer, less easy to read signs like when Neil and I, sitting by our traditional end of the day spring campfire, make eye contact and knowingly nod. It's show time- the woodcock are flying and the grouse are drumming. It's one thing to catch the woodcock silhouetted against a fading sunset it's another to do it at the exact instant a grouse starts drumming in a nearby thicket. This is the show we wait for every spring. Perfect timing, a simultaneous treat for ear and eye. A fortunate coincidence, perhaps, but we prefer to think of it as something more. To us it's a sign, a signal that things are as they should be. We have done right by the grouse and woodcock and this one special evening they have teamed up to return the favor. Our habitat work has been paid in full and then some. If you could put a tape measure on satisfaction this one would more than make the book. Leopold writes, "When land does well for its owner and the owner does well by his land we have conservation". Now, that's something to talk about!

Visitors to our campfire are thrilled by the sight and sound of the spring woodcock and grouse. They appreciate the significance of what they have just witnessed but they don't seem to be able to feel it as we do. They have not had a hand in creating the grouse's secret drumming spots or the woodcock's feeding flat. They didn't sweat over saw and log, they didn't dig the worming bog. And, because they didn't touch the land, they are mere spectators. They are denied the deep, impossible to describe, feeling of completeness and inner satisfaction that comes from knowing that you have done something right by your land and it is responding in kind.

I have learned that the stiff joints and achy muscles which come from running a dozer or bush hog for six straight hours is merely a reminder that something good has just happened, not a sign of old age or failing health. I love nothing more than to gaze out upon a three-acre food plot and the dozen or so deer it feeds each night. The feeling is both comforting and exhilirating at the same time. I have had a hand in that. I have done something right. I feel a kind of inner peace and satisfaction a "soft" sense of accomplishment the likes of which can never be delivered by measuring deer antlers. I am experiencing first hand, the love, respect, and admiration for the land that Leopold writes about in his famous essay "The Land Ethic". And I am not alone, Neil feels the same way and so does our hunting partner Steve who was so overtaken with deer management that he went out and bought not one but two old, grown-over, farms to practice habitat management on with his dad and son. And there are hundreds of thousands more of us out there including almost the entire membership of the Quality Deer Management Association. We have connected to the land and in doing so have connected to each other. Are we are becoming a "secret society of land stewards"?

I came to Leopold later than most. I managed to escape college without reading so much as a page of Leopold's most popular work *A Sand County Almanac*. I had consumed virtually everything written on Quality Deer Management and habitat improvement before I ever encountered his books and essays. But after the first page I was hooked, wildlife poetry embedded in management prose; a philosophy of life, superimposed upon a land ethic. After years of searching I had finally found a way to make sense of my attraction to land and the spell land seemed to have over me. Leopold connects the dots between hunting, Native American spirituality, and land stewardship. For years I knew they were connected; I just couldn't figure out how or for that matter, why. The more involved I became with my property and the more I learned about wildlife habitat management, the more sense Leopold made to me. His principles of wildlife management are as on target today as they were seventy years ago but, his land ethic philosophy that has kept my compass set true north.

Through most of his professional career Aldo Leopold worked aggressively to reverse a number of destructive land management trends. At the top of his list was the demise of the small, family owned farm and the trend toward large-scale agribusiness. Leopold saw ag colleges and county ag extensions encouraging farmers to increase productivity by clearing land, draining wetlands, eliminating hedgerows and otherwise eliminating acres of wildlife habitat. He argued passionately that small landowners should resist these practices and continue to provide for wildlife by leaving some of their lands in an "unimproved" state. Leopold virtually pleaded with private landowners to "do right" by the land and the wildlife who inhabit it by retaining the small farm landscapes prevalent at the turn of the twentieth century. These landscapes resembled ragged patchwork quilts of fields and woodlands and grown over places.

He argued for a moratorium on the elimination of field hedgerows. The more overgrown the hedgerow, the better he liked it. Birds, rabbits and all sorts of critters called hedgerows home and he believed it was little enough to leave them intact. Leopold also believed field edges, corners, and end-of-field turnarounds should be left to wildlife. Who would ever miss an acre or two of grown up field that could become home to a needy covey of quail? Draining wetlands to create cropland was an enormous waste of waterfowl and winter pheasant habitat. Streams should be allowed to meander and be skirted with nest building brush while ponds benefited both man and beast alike.

Make no mistake; Leopold wasn't anti progress or anti agriculture, not at all. He was far from the preservationists of today with their touch nothing do nothing mantra. He was a realist who understood that good things could happen when people and land came together and took care of each other. He often referred to this "give and get" relationship between land and people as "conservation"

Unfortunately much of Leopold's message fell on deaf ears. At least on the deaf ears of the small farmers and landowners of the thirties and forties who believed they were faced with going under or changing their farming practices. Leopold's argument of leaving something for wildlife was a tough one to swallow when there were mouths to feed, especially with the professional agriculture community touting large-scale agribusiness practices as the salvation of the farming industry. Wildlife and the land are the big losers. Economics-- the ultimate American trump card.

Leopold was one of the earliest deer managers to address deer overpopulation issues. While others called for more deer to hunt, overpopulation issues. While others called for more deer to hunt, he cautioned that overpopulation was leading to habitat destruction. Woodlands cannot regenerate when pastured by deer (or cattle for that matter). He was an early advocate of harvesting does and balancing deer herds.

Fast-forward a half-century plus. Today, deer are big business. Hundreds of thousands of deer hunters are creating quality deer hunting on lands they lease or own by following the science and philosophy of the Quality Deer Management Association. Whitetail habitat management is "de rigueur" for serious whitetail hunters. Hunter-landowners are suddenly becoming farmers and people of the land. They are buying tractors and seeders and hiring wildlife consultants and they are doing it right. Leopold Landscapes are appearing everywhere white-tailed deer and deer hunters are found. Big bucks are being spent on big bucks. Leopold has become not only relevant but also real. Once again economics is the driver; this time wildlife and land finally win big.

When we acquired our property fifteen years ago it was a mere ghost of the farm complex it had been at the turn of the twentieth century. The farm had grown up into three hundred and fifty acres of mixed hardwood forest and another hundred and fifty acres of thick pole timber trying to become hardwood forest. There were no open spaces left on the property, and the wooded areas showed serious signs of over utilization by deer. The property hadn't seen a plow or mower in fifty years or more. Succession was delayed in some areas due to some livestock pasturing and deer browsing but even the pasture areas were well on their way to becoming pole timber. Bottom line, we had too much standing timber, not enough edge and very few wildlife openings. It was a far cry from the Leopold Landscape it had been one hundred years earlier.

The solution could have come right from Leopold. Create more food and cover by clearing, planting, cutting and creating spaces where different habitat types intersect. Open up ten or so miles log trails and plant with wildlife forage mixes. Clear old log landings

and grown over fields to create thirty acres of food plots. Release some thirty-five old apple and pear trees. Thin timber stands, and harvest mature timber to encourage acorn production and regeneration. Clear-cut fifteen to twenty acres of hard woods for cover and browse. Sounds simple, but it took time, backbreaking work, and regular outlays of cash for equipment, seed, and lime and fertilizer. It's all presented in our book.

It took motivation; but boy were we motivated! At first we were motivated by visions of big bucks on food plots and hunting like we read about in magazines but have never experienced ourselves. Wish I could say it was for the good of the land or some sort of Black Elk spiritual connection but I can't. Our primary goal, plain and simple, was to create a great place to hunt deer; a place to see mature bucks on every hunt and harvest some high quality animals.

Becoming good land stewards and intensifying our connection with the land came later. It was an unexpected yet welcome by-product of the work we did in the name of creating quality deer hunting and the influence of Aldo Leopold. Over time, developing a land ethic became more and more important to us. We liked the feeling of well being we got when we did right by our land and we wanted more. Without our knowing it, the means had become the end.

Leopold's message is as relevant today as it has ever been. In fact the economic, ecological, and quality deer management planets have aligned themselves to create an environment of "Leopold reality" like never before. Failing farm economics made Leopold's message irrelevant seventy years ago. Today, the economics of quality deer and quality deer hunting has created a new world of relevance. Readers of this book will do well to acquaint themselves with Aldo Leopold. His teachings will give the good work you are doing direction, relevance and passion.

"Something's Happening Here"
an Essay by Craig Dougherty

"Something" happens when hunters start working with the land. The "something" comes gradually; and sort of sneaks up on you. By the time you realize what's happening it's too late. It starts with a vague sense that something good is happening; something more than finally having finished a job. You look at your work; take a deep breath and wonder. Will it work? Have I done harm? Will wildlife benefit from what I have done?

Time passes and you realize that you have done no harm. In fact, you've done well. Done well by the land and done well by the wildlife that depends on it. Your confidence grows. You get comfortable. You begin to develop an overall feeling of well being. It feels right. It feels good. Something's happening here. You are doing well by your land and, your land is doing well by you. You have entered into philosophical sphere of Aldo Leopold.

In the end you find yourself putting the land before all else; where your land was once a means to an end, it is now the end in and of itself. The hunt has almost become secondary. For some of us it occasionally is secondary. You are hooked on land stewardship. The more you give the more is returned in kind. If you leave the land for more than a few days you feel an irrational need to get back. It calls to you. You feel good when you are there; you feel whole. You are hooked on land!

Leopold knew this feeling well and wrote eloquently about it. He helped us understand what we were experiencing with our land and how to share this special experience with others. It is our hope that an awareness of Aldo Leopold and his beliefs gives us a better understanding of the importance of connecting with the land and developing a true land ethic. Leopold gives us a truer sense of purpose by putting our work in its proper ecological context. It's more than just antlers.

We urge our readers to embrace this notion and to share this perspective with others. Our deer management endeavors are not without their critics. Our critics need to know that it is more than big deer and big antlers; it's also about land. We speak frequently of deer yet seldom of stewardship. It's easier to speak of deer than of the land; this is a new conversation for many of us. But nonetheless, speak we must. Too often we speak of stewardship in hushed tones around late night campfires. The deer stories told; we reach deep within ourselves and reflect. We speak in half sentences and knowing nods, transfixed by deep seeded feelings and the campfire. We speak of the land; but we do not shout.

The public once inextricably linked hunters with conservation and conservation causes. Hunters protected wildlife and supplied much needed monies for habitat and wildlife restoration. But, the story has faded with time. Happily a new chapter is being written today. . Hunters practicing Quality Deer Management are creating millions of acres of "Leopold Landscapes". They are leaving big, broad, stewardship footprints wherever whitetails are found and the land is better for it. Somthing's definitely happening here. Be proud of what we do, tell our story with conviction and be heard.

The Original "Kindred Spirits"

Illustration by Michael Ancillotti

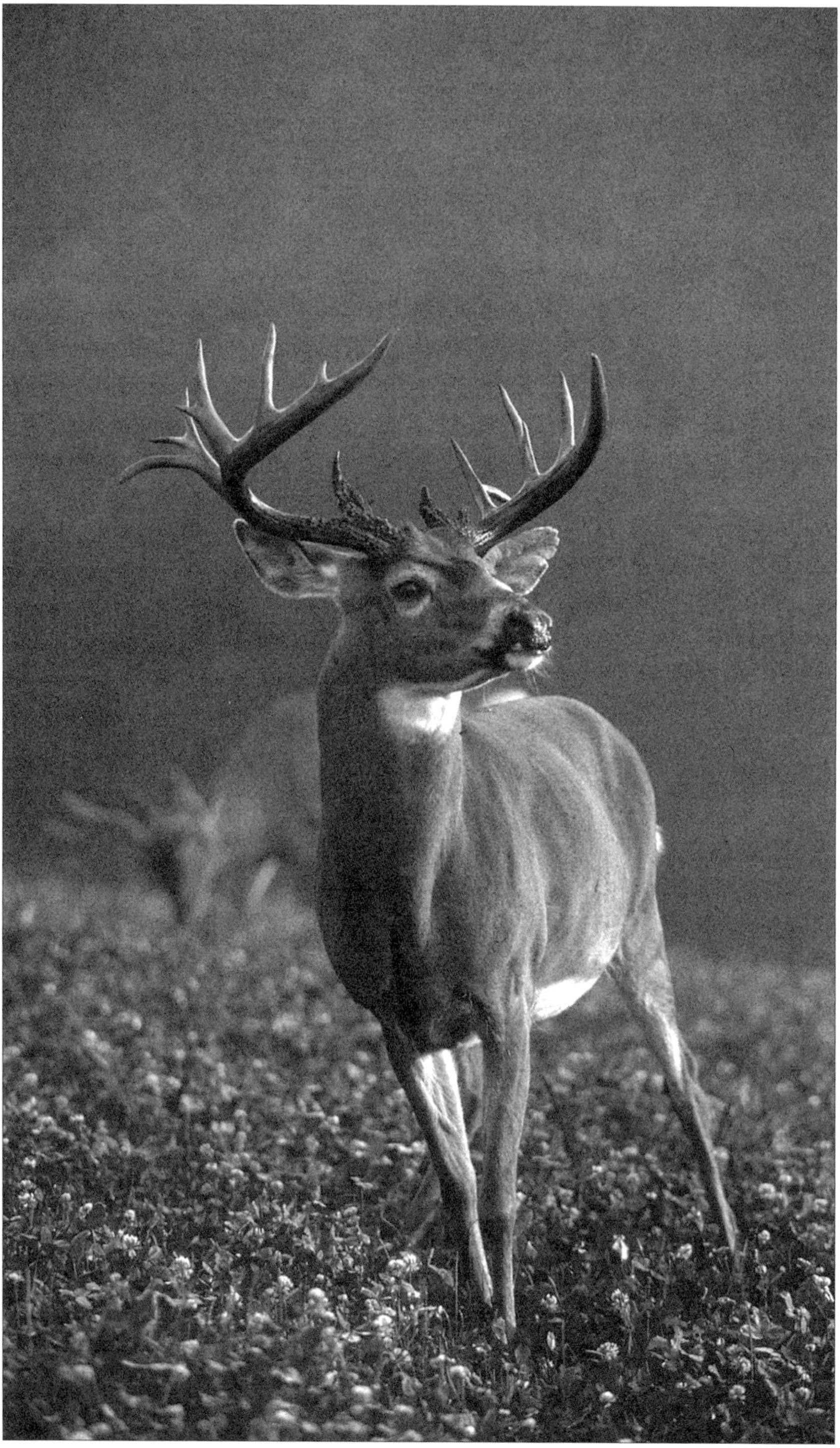

Photo by Charles J. Alsheimer

NOTES

NOTES

Afterward

NOTES

NOTES

GIVE THE GIFT OF

NorthCountry Whitetails
Reference Guides to Creating
Habitat and Wildlife Food Plots

To Your Hunting Friends, Club Members and Local Library.

❑ YES, I want ___ copies of *Grow 'Em Right, A Guide to Creating Habitat and Food Plots, Revised Edition* for $19.95 ea.

❑ YES, I want _____ copies of *Plant 'Em Right, How to Create Wildlife Food Plots, Revised Edition DVD* for $19.95 ea.

❑ YES, I am interested in having Neil Dougherty speak or give a seminar to my organization. Please send information.

Include $5.05 shipping and handling for one book or DVD, and $2.00 for each additional book or DVD. New York residents must include applicable sales tax. Canadian orders must include payment in US funds.

Payment must accompany order. Allow 3 weeks for delivery.

My check or money order for $ _____ is enclosed.
Please charge my ❑Visa ❑MasterCard ❑Discover

Name _____
Organization _____
Address _____
City/State/Zip _____
Phone _____ Email _____
Card # _____
Exp. Date _____
Signature _____

For Faster Service
CALL **315-331-6959**
Order online at
www.NorthCountryWhitetails.com